Alexander James Duffield

**Peru in the Guano Age**

Being a short account of a recent visit to the guano deposits, with some reflections on the money they have produced and the uses to which it has been applied

Alexander James Duffield

**Peru in the Guano Age**
*Being a short account of a recent visit to the guano deposits, with some reflections on the money they have produced and the uses to which it has been applied*

ISBN/EAN: 9783337384227

Printed in Europe, USA, Canada, Australia, Japan

Cover: Foto ©ninafisch / pixelio.de

More available books at **www.hansebooks.com**

# PERU IN THE GUANO AGE

BEING A SHORT

## ACCOUNT OF A RECENT VISIT

TO THE

## GUANO DEPOSITS

WITH SOME

REFLECTIONS ON THE MONEY THEY HAVE PRODUCED AND
THE USES TO WHICH IT HAS BEEN APPLIED

BY

A. J. DUFFIELD

LONDON
RICHARD BENTLEY AND SON
Publishers in Ordinary to Her Majesty the Queen
1877

# DEDICATORY LETTER.

Á

Señor Don Juan Espinosa y de Maldonado,

*Estimado y distinguido Amigo mio:*

It would be most pleasant to continue this letter in the language in which it begins and which you taught me some five and twenty years ago, but I wish others to read it as well as yourself.

I dedicate this little book to you for several reasons: not because of our common friendship, extending now over more than a quarter of a century, nor yet for the confidence which you have reposed in me under many trying circumstances during that long period, but rather because you are much interested in the country which the book describes, are intimately acquainted with all the questions it raises, and more than all because you have a thorough knowledge of Peru—its people and history;—because further, it was you who first taught me how to regard your countrymen, opened my eyes to their good and other qualities, and because also you know that here I have set down nought in malice, have said nothing that you do not know to be true, and drawn no inference from the facts of past times or the doings of living men which you would not sanction and endorse.

With one exception.

I am quite aware that you do not share in what I have said at page 118, but this is not my own opinion—it is the candidly expressed view of the leading men of Lima. I know that you have always insisted upon Peru paying her debts, not merely because you well know that she can pay quite easily, but also because the effect on the moral life of the country, if she should prove a defaulter, will be most disastrous. It is pitiable beyond the power of human expression to find a single thoughtful Peruvian holding a contrary opinion.

Since the following chapters were written several things have taken place which have corroborated some of my statements, and fulfilled more than one of my predictions. As you are aware a public meeting was held, a month after my departure from Lima, at the Treasurer's Office; at which were present the Minister of Finance and Commerce, the Chief Accountant, and many other officers of departments, for the purpose of receiving a communication from two Englishmen, setting forth the discovery of fresh guano deposits on the coast, in the province of Tarapaca. From all that could be gathered these new deposits may be fairly estimated as containing three million tons of guano. This confirms what I have said at page 101.

And yet we have heard nothing new from Peru regarding the payment of her liabilities, nor has any official communication been made by the Government regarding this important discovery. If General Prado does not take care he will have his house pulled about his ears. One of the most interesting revolutions yet to be made in Peru is one in the interest of its honour and uprightness. If your friend General Montero appeals to the country in that cause he might immortalize his name and bring in the New Era. From the little I know of the General, however, I should say that such a task is too much for him. It requires a man broad of chest, of constant mind, of unimpeachable honour and absolute unselfishness to make a revolution of that sort. Still it is a good cry, and if Prado does not take it up himself he may come to grief when he least expects it.

By the issue of Mr. Marsh's report from the British Consulate at Callao you will notice how the Consul confirms what I have said about the British sailor in Peru. Excessive drinking, licentious living, and exposure are set forth as the main causes of a deterioration in our merchant seamen which should attract the notice of Parliament. To send unseaworthy ships to sea is to bring disgrace on the national name. The national disgrace of sending unworthy seamen to sea appears to attract little notice.

The chapter I read to you in MS. on 'Commercial Enterprise in Peru' I have purposely omitted, as also my report on the riches of its Sea. It will be time enough to talk of these things when the Chinese get a firmer footing in the country than they have at present, or when the Mormons have established themselves there.

Let me ask you to treat with leniency any unintentional wrong thinking or wrong writing, but anything you discover here to be purposely vulgar, purposely bad, or unjust, treat it as you would treat the creed of a Jesuit, or a priest, or any other evil thing.

    Believe me to be,
      My dear Don Juan,
        Your faithful friend and servant,
           Q. B. S. M.
         A. J. DUFFIELD.

SAVILE CLUB,
 *February*, 1877.


P. S. Let me publicly thank you for introducing to English readers the works of RICARDO PALMA, certainly the best writer Peru has produced, and eminently its first satirist. As you will see, I have translated one of his *Tradiciones*. Some readers at first sight might naturally feel inclined to suggest a transposition of the chapters in the 'Law-suit against God,' or to look upon the second chapter as altogether irrelevant to the story. But we who are in the secret know better, and that the official corruption which is there set forth is intimately connected with the catastrophe which follows, and is a faithful representation of public life and morals, not only in old Peru, but also in the Peru of the Guano Age.

        *Hasta cada rata.*

# PERU IN THE GUANO AGE.

## CHAPTER I.

ALTHOUGH Peru may boast of its Age of Guano, it has had its Golden Age. This was before any Spaniard had put his foot in the country, and when as yet it was called by quite another name. The name of Peru, which signifies nothing, arose by accident or mistake. It was first of all spelled Piru, no doubt from Biru, the native name of one of its rivers. Time and use, which establish so many things, have established Peru; and it is too late to think of disestablishing it for anything else: and though it is nothing to boast of, let Peru stand. The country had its Stone Age, and I have brought for the Cambridge antiquaries a fair collection of implements of that period, consisting of lancets, spear-heads, and heads for arrows, exquisitely wrought in flint, jasper, opal, chalcedony, and other stones. They were all found in the neighbourhood of the Pisagua river. It is to be regretted that no material evidence of equal tangibility is forthcoming of the Age of Gold. This is generally the result of comparison founded on historical criticism.

In the Golden Age Peru had—

I. A significant name, a well-ordered, fixed, and firm government, with hereditary rulers. Only one rebellion occurred in twelve reigns, and only two revolutions are recorded in the whole history of the Inca Empire.

II. The land was religiously cultivated.

III. There was a perfect system of irrigation, and water was made the servant and slave of man.

IV. The land was equally divided periodically between the Deity, the Inca, the nobles, and the people.

V. Strong municipal laws enforced, and an intelligent and vigorous administration carried out these laws, which provided for cleanliness, health, and order.

VI. Idleness was punished as a crime; work abounded for all; and no one could want, much less starve.

VII. No lawsuit could last longer, or its decision be delayed more, than five days.

VIII. Throughout the land the people everywhere were taught such industrial arts as were good and useful, and were also trained by a regular system of bodily exercises for purposes of health, and the defence of the nation.

IX. Every male at a certain age married, and took upon himself the duties of citizenship and the responsibilities of a manly life: he owned his own house and lived in it, and a portion of land fell to him every year, which was enlarged as his family increased.

X. Great public works were every year built which added to the strength and glory of the kingdom.

XI. Deleterious occupations or such as were injurious to health were prohibited.

XII. Gold was used for ornament, sacred vessels of the temple, and the service of the Inca in his palaces. There is a tradition that this precious metal signified in their tongue '*Tears of the Sun.*' Whether this be an ancient or a modern tradition no one can tell us. It may be not more than three and a half centuries old.

XIII. A man ravishing a virgin was buried alive.

XIV. A man ravishing a virgin of the Sun, that is, one of the vestal virgins of the Temple, was burnt alive.

XV. It was accounted infamous for a man or woman to wear other people's clothes, or clothes that were in rags.

XVI. Roads and bridges were among the foremost public works which bound the vast country together.

XVII. Public granaries, for the storing of corn in case of emergency, were erected in all parts, and some very out-of-the-way parts of the kingdom.

XVIII. Woollen and cotton manufactures were brought to great perfection. Examples of these remain to this day and will bear comparison with those of our own time.

XIX. A thief suffered the loss of his eyes;

and a creature committing the diabolical act of altering a water-course suffered death.

And to sum up, here is the true confession of Mancio Sierra Lejesama, one of the first Spanish Conquistadores of Peru, which confession he attached to his will made in the city of Cuzco on the 15th day of September, 1589, before one Geronimo Sanches de Quesada, escribano publico, and which has been preserved to us by Espinosa in his 'People's Dictionary,' art. 'Indio.'

'First of all,' says the dying Lejesama, 'before commencing my will I declare that I have much desired in all submission to acquaint His Catholic Majesty, the King Don Philip our Lord, seeing how Catholic and Christian he is, and how jealous for the service of God our Saviour, of what touches the discharge of my soul for the great part I took in the discovery, conquest, and peopling of these kingdoms, when we took them from those who were their masters, the Incas, who owned and ruled them as their own kingdoms, and put them under the royal crown. And His Catholic Majesty shall understand that the said Incas governed these kingdoms on such wise that in them all there was no thief or vicious person, nor an idle man, nor a bad or an adulterous woman, [if such there had been, be sure the Spaniard would have been the first to find it out,] nor were there allowed among them people of evil lives: men had their honest and profitable occupations, in all that pertained to mountain or mine, to the field, the forest, or the home, as in everything of use all was governed and divided after such sort that each one knew and held to his own without another interfering therewith: nor were lawsuits known among them: the affairs of war, although not few, interfered not with those of traffic, nor yet did these conflict with those of seed-time and harvest, or with other matters whatsoever. All things from the greater to the less had their order, concert, and good management. The Incas were dreaded, obeyed, and respected by their subjects, for the greatness of their capacity and the excellence of their rule. It was the same with the captains and governors of provinces. And as we found command, and strength, and force to rest in these, so had we to deprive them of these by the force of arms to subject them to, and press them into, the service of God our Lord, taking from them not only all command but their means of life also. And by the permission of God our Lord we were able to subject this kingdom of many people, and riches, and lords, making servants of them as now we see. I trust that His Majesty understands the motive which moves me to this relation, that it is for the purging of my conscience by the confession of my guilt. We have destroyed with our evil example people so well governed as these, who were so far from being inclined to wrongdoing or excess of any sort—both men and women—that an Indian with a hundred thousand dollars in gold and silver in his house, would leave it open, or would place a broom, or small stick across the threshold to signify that the owner was not within, and with that, as was their custom, no one would enter, nor take thence a single thing. When they saw us put doors to our houses, and locks on our doors, they understood that we were afraid of them, not that they would kill us, but that perhaps they might steal our things. When they saw that we had thieves among ourselves, and men who incited their wives and daughters to sin, they held us in low esteem. So great is the dissoluteness now among these natives, and their offences against God, owing to the evil example we have set them in all things, that from doing nothing bad they have all—or nearly all—been converted in our day into those who can do nothing good. This touches also His Majesty, who will take care that his conscience has no part in allowing these things to continue. With this I implore God to pardon me, Who has moved me to declare these matters, because I am the last to die of all the discoverers and conquistadores; for it is notorious that now there exists not one other of their number, but I only either in this kingdom or out of it, and with that I rest, having done all I am able for the discharge of my conscience.'

This might be called the epitaph of the Golden Age, written by one who knew it, and who helped to destroy it.

XX. Hospitality was a passion in that time, and what had been enjoined and practised as a national duty became a private virtue, procuring intense happiness in its exercise. Instances of this are on record that are not equalled in the history of any other people.

Lastly — and these characteristics of our Golden Age have been taken quite at random and as they have come to my recollection—the name by which the Incas most delighted themselves in being known was that of 'Lovers of the Poor.' In this Golden Age gunpowder was unknown, and the people for the most part were vegetarians. Animal food was eaten by the soldiery and the labouring people only at the great religious feasts. Fish, and the flesh of alpacas, were confined to the Incas and the nobles. This will account for many things which subsequently occurred, notably their easy conquest by the fire- and meat-eating Spaniard.

Let us now write down our comparisons of the Age of Guano with the Age of Gold.

I. The name and form of Government, it is true, are reduced to writing, but the Government is, and has been from the commencement of its Republican history, as unstable as water. On the close of the Guano Age things would appear to be improving: President Pardo has completed the whole term of his presidential life, and this is only the second instance of a Peruvian Republican President having done so. It would be difficult to reckon up the number of revolutions which have taken place in the Age of Manure.

II. The land is not cultivated: the things, for the most part, which are taken to market, are those which grow spontaneously, without art or industry. The people who supply the Lima market are chiefly Italians, while the greater part of the land is barren and unproductive. Potatoes and other vegetables, wheat and barley, flour, fruits, and beef, all come from Chile and Equador, but chiefly from the former.

III. The great water-courses and system of irrigation which marked the Golden Age are all broken up, and the fructifying water, once stored for the use and service of man, first became his master, and then his relentless tyrant.

IV. The land cannot be said to belong to any one. Certainly not to God. Even the Church, once a great proprietor and holder of slaves, is as lazy as the laziest drone in any known hive. Many of the large estates which flourished in the pre-Guano period have perished for lack of hands. The sugar plantations are exceptions for the present, but what will happen to them when the Chinese are all free is very uncertain. It may even be said to be a source of alarm to many thoughtful persons.

V. Of the municipal laws, which provide for cleanliness, health, and public order, although great progress has been made in Central Lima, all that need be said is, that it is a wonder the inhabitants have survived, and that those who were not killed in last year's revolution have not been carried off by a plague.

VI. Idleness among the upper classes, i.e. the whole white population, the descendants of Spain—those who supply the Army and Navy with officers, the Law with judges, the Church with bishops, and the rich daughters of sugar-boilers with husbands—idleness among these is the order of the day, and is punished by no one. Even the gods appear to take no notice of it, being itself a sort of god, so far as the number of his worshippers are concerned. To-morrow is the everlasting excuse for almost everybody, and yesterday has done nothing but light fools to dusty death; the to-morrow in which the useful and the good are to be done, never comes.

VII. Going to law is not only an infamous passion in this Guano Age, it is a means of living. There must be few if any people of substance in Peru who have not known the bitter curse of the law's delay. I have known lawsuits of the most vexatious and cruel nature, and which, in any country where civilisation is not a mere name, could never have been instituted, last, not five days, but five years, and, alas! even fifteen years. I have myself tasted the bitterness of the law in this land, and been very near being lodged in a loathsome jail at the instance of a miscreant who had it in his power to demand my presence before a bribe-gorged judge. I only escaped paying heavy toll or hateful imprisonment by my friends obtaining the removal of the judge. The second was a gross attempt at extortion, from which I was saved by accident. Both these lawsuits, of the basest sort, had their origin in an injustice which is ingrained in the complexion of the people. The captain and crew of the *Talisman* could bear testimony to the difference between the administration of law in the Golden Age and in the Age of Manure.

VIII. The education of the people has never been seriously attempted, except in carrying a flimsy old musket. The Indians, who form the great bulk of the population, do not vote. This would involve a slight cultivation of the Indian's intellect, and he does not know what might happen to further embitter his lot if he were to discover to his rulers that he had a mind. He is perhaps the slyest of animals—

more sly than a fox, more obstinate than an English mule, and as timid as a squirrel.

IX. The marriage law is disgracefully abused and neglected for a country which boasts that its religion is that of the Holy Roman Apostolical. Civil marriage is illegal, and ecclesiastical marriage but little observed, except among the Estratocracia, the sugar-boilers, and such as mix in European society. The subject is one always difficult for a traveller to handle. To speak plainly and publicly of what has been acquired in private on this matter would justly provoke displeasure and disgust, and would not fail to be misrepresented or misunderstood. It may, however, be said, that if marriage be a public virtue, large numbers of the Peruvians of the Manure Age are not virtuous.

X. Of the great public works in Peru, the chief during this time has been a penitentiary, and a railway to the moon not yet finished, all built by foreigners and with English money. Emigration was one of the most important transactions of the Golden Age. There has been no serious attempt at promoting either emigration or immigration: the migration of the native races is absolutely beyond the control of the government.

XI. Of deleterious occupations and

XII. The use of gold, all that need be said is that each man in Peru does what he likes in his own eyes, and what is allowed in the most enlightened land under the sun: and in this regard she sins in the universal company of the wide world; but the comparison with the Golden Age is not on that account the less painful.

XIII. Incontinence is general, and the number of illegitimate children greater than those born in wedlock. The crime punishable by the terrible death awarded to it in the Golden Age has disappeared, for reasons which need not be further noticed.

XIV. The scandals of the Temple or the Church have likewise changed in their character. I have known a bishop of the Peruvian State Church, sworn to celibacy, whose illegitimate children were more numerous than the years of his life. I have known a parish priest who had living in several houses more than thirty children by several women. All Peruvian ecclesiastics are supposed to live celibate lives, bishops, priests, monks and nuns; and if they do not, the irregularity is winked at, nor is public morality shocked, however grossly and notoriously immoral the lives of these persons may be.

XV. The people for the most part are well dressed, but with the exception of the indigenous races, all wear ready-made clothing. The dresses of all classes are ill-made, costly, and vulgar. The coffin in which a Peruvian of the Guano Period is carried to his last home, is about the best made suit he ever wears, and the best fitting.

XVI. Of roads and bridges of the present day, it would be amusing to write if the recollection of those I have passed over was not too painful. No man not born in an Age of Manure, who has travelled a thousand miles in the interior of Peru, or for that matter a hundred leagues, will ever wish to repeat the experiment. Many of these roads are but ruins of roads, and carry the usual aspect of roads which lead to ruin.

XVII. There are no public granaries. People live from hand to mouth on what others grow for them and bring to them.

XVIII. There are no woollen manufactories.

All the wool of the alpaca, the llama, and vicuña is sent to England to be made into things which the growers of the staple never see, much less wear. No Peruvian of any social standing has had the pluck or the sense to do anything towards extending the cultivation of alpaca wool. It is well known that the produce of this beautiful and docile animal might easily have been increased, just as the yield of merino wool has increased in Australia, if only brains and industry had been brought to bear upon the enterprise; and instead of a yearly income of a few thousand dollars being derived from this source of national wealth, there might have been, within the limits of the Age of Guano, a net annual income of £20,000,000. This incredible statement is made by one who passed four years of his life in studying the subject.

XIX. As for stealing—not that form of it which comes within the range of petty larceny, but the wider and more awful range of felony—it may be safely said, that nearly all public men have steeped themselves to the neck in this crime, and the common people take to it as easily and naturally as birds in a garden take to sweet berries. Nor is there sufficient justice in the country to stamp out the offence.

If the punishment awarded to this crime in the Golden Age had been inflicted in the Age of Guano, there would be a very limited sale for spectacles in Lima or the cities of the Peruvian coast, or the towns and cities of the mountains.

XX. It is delightful to turn to something in Peru that merits unlimited praise. The Golden Age was noted for its hospitality, not only as a social virtue practised by the people among themselves, but as extended to strangers. Pizarro had not been so successful in his conquest of Peru if he had not been so hospitably treated by the noble lady who entertained him on his first visit to Tumbez. The exhortation of Huayna Capac to his subjects to receive the bearded men—whose advent he announced—as superior beings, has been interpreted as the cause of the Spaniards' sudden success in a country that was well defended as well by soldiers as numerous fortresses—'Those words,' exclaimed an Inca noble some years afterwards, 'those last words of Inca Huayna Capac were our conquerors.' Among themselves it was the custom to eat their meals with open doors, and any passer by in need was welcomed in. Princesses and high-born ladies received visits from the mothers and daughters of the people, who provided the needle-work that was to occupy the time of the visit. Among English families of the better sort it is still a habit for a lady visitor to ask for some needle-work to do during her visit if it lasts more than a day— a custom that deserves to be enquired into. The prevalence of a similar custom in our Golden Age increases its importance. The traveller, especially if he be an Englishman, who has travelled through modern Peru, even in the Guano Age, who does not bear a lively recollection of kindness and open-hearted hospitality, is most certainly to be pitied, if not avoided. I am quite aware that such persons exist. I have myself travelled in the saddle more than two thousand miles on less than as many pence. The story of the impostor Arthur Orton at Melipilla is a case in point, and if the learned counsel who defended him is in need of a livelihood which cannot dispense with some of the elegances and charms of life, he cannot do better than follow the tracks of his client. I have lived in every kind of house, rancho, posta, cottage, quinta, and mansion, occupied by the various classes which make up the population of Peru. I have lived with archbishops and bishops, priests and monks, merchant princes, senators, judges, generals, miners, doctors, professional thieves, and widows, and I should be an ingrate indeed if I did not acknowledge with profound gratitude the kindness, oftentimes the affection, which I received, the liberality with which I was entertained, and the freedom I enjoyed. Here I am reminded of an incident which occurred to me in the south of Spain, and as it will suit a purpose it could not otherwise serve, let me relate it.

I was employed to take the level of a railway that was to connect the Roblé with the shores of the Mediterranean. The proposed line passed through one of the great estates of the Marquis de Blanco, and the Marquis gave me a letter to his capitaz or overseer, who occupied a house, the sight of which would have charmed the soul of an artist, on one of the overhanging cliffs which rose above el Rio Verde. I arrived late and after twelve hours hard work beneath an Andalusian sun. I was well received by the capitaz and his charming wife Doña Carmen, who with her own hands and in my presence prepared for my supper a partridge and other delightful things. If the day had been hot, the night on the highest point of the royal road to Ronda was cold. A glorious wood fire added to the universal beauty of everything. A table was spread for me with a snowy diaper cloth. I can see it now—a bottle of fine wine, most sweet bread, raisins and what not. Just as my partridge was ready, a clatter of twenty horses' hoofs was heard in the patio. The capitaz went out to see the new arrivals, who turned out to be farmers of the district on their way to the horse fair, which was to be held in Ronda the following day. In came the twenty pilgrims to Ronda, to whom I was formally introduced, and Doña Carmen set to work to prepare an enormous *Olla* for the whole company. My partridge was not served until the *Olla* was ready, when we all set to work and ate our supper in peace and good-will. An hour afterwards, whether from the effects of the delightful wine—only to be enjoyed in Spain, the fumes of my own pipe and the cigarettes of the twenty pilgrims, the labours of the day, or all combined, I fell a nodding: whereupon the good-natured capitaz enquired if I would not like to throw myself into bed. On which I rose, and declared with great solemnity that for my rudeness in having gone to sleep in such worshipful company, I was ready to throw myself not only into bed but into the river below.

'Doña Carmen,' said the capitaz, 'shall take you to your room.'

And with a general good-night to the pilgrims and a shake of the hand with the capitaz, away I went in the wake of Doña Carmen.

It was a spacious room, filled with implements of sport, the walls adorned with heads of deer and other trophies of the gun, and there were also unmistakeable signs of its being a lady's room.

'Doña Carmen,' I observed in an imperative tone, 'this is your own room. I am an old traveller, and can sleep in a hay-loft or on the floor, with my saddle for a pillow. At any rate, I will not sleep here. I will not turn you out of your own room.'

'And,' she demanded, 'what would the Marquis say if he knew that you had slept here in the hay-loft or on the floor, with your saddle for a pillow?'

Other expostulations followed, which were answered with great eloquence and stately determination, mixed with that grave humour which can no more be acquired than can be acquired the wearing of a cloak as it is worn by an ancient hidalgo, or the arrangement of a mantilla as it is arranged on the head and shoulders of a high-born lady of Granada.

At last, as I caught up my satchel to leave the room, she caught me by the arm, and nudging me with her elbow, she said with much archness, 'I am coming back again,' and with that she swept out of the room, leaving me no longer with my eyes half closed in sleep.

She never came back. Nor did I ever see her again. She never intended to come back. Those who think so are incapable of making or understanding a joke, and will never be able to appreciate the uncommon wit and humour of Spanish women. That there are shallow fools in the world who interpret everything they hear in a carnal and literal sense is the reason why we have so many childish, not to say unpleasant, stories from Spain and Peru regarding the questionable morals of the fair sex of those countries. What is meant for fun and drollery is mistaken for naughtiness, and much that is offered as a spontaneous natural hospitality has been wilfully or ignorantly misconstrued. I do not defend the method Doña Carmen took in putting her guest at his ease, and making him feel at home; I think it was a daring act of politeness, and it is not pretty to find so much knowledge of the world in the possession of a woman, however dexterous her use of it may be. There is, however, another kind of culture besides that which comes from reading expensive novels, dressing for church or dinner, and living in a climate somewhat cold, foggy, and changeable. The ladies of Peru are beautiful, natural, very intelligent, and fond of living an unconstrained life. Their climate is provocative of freedom, ease, and delightful idleness. Their fair speech and delightful wit partake of these characteristics. It is born of these. It can be misinterpreted—but only by those who know not their language, and do not respect their ways.

A common source of error on the subject of Peruvian hospitality arises from the fact that in Lima, for example, a foreigner, even an Englishman, is rarely or never invited to dine with a native family. With us, if we meet a man in Bond Street, or anywhere on the wing, whom we have not seen for a year, we ask him to come and take pot-luck with us, and if he is a foreigner he generally does—and notwithstanding the detestable anxiety of our wives, our pot-luck dinners are the best dinners that we give. What is lacking in the mutton we can and often do make up with the bottle or the pipe. This is the kind of thing we expect in return when we visit Lima and pick up a man who has thus dined with us at home. But the thing is impossible. In Lima a married man dines with his grandmother, his wife's grandmother, his wife's father and mother, together with his wife and the children, whom the old people love to spoil with sugar-plums. The ladies are only half dressed, the service is somewhat slatternly, the dishes, although excellent in their way, are such as do not please the weak stomachs of benighted Englishmen, much less the French, who have not made the acquaintance of the puchero, the ajijaco, or the omnipresent dulces. In short, a stranger at a Peruvian family dinner, unexpected and without a formal preparation, would be as acceptable as a dog at Mass. And when an Englishman is invited to one of these houses he never forgets the things done in his honour —the loads of dishes—the floods of wine—the magnificent dresses of the ladies—the elaborate display of everything;—and oh! the stately coldness, the searching of dark eyes, and the awful sense of responsibility which rests on the being for whom all this has been done, and who is the solitary cause of it all. He never accepts another invitation. And yet the people have strained every nerve to please him; they have made themselves ill, have spent an awful sum of money, and less and less believe in dining a man as the most perfect form of showing him their respect or esteem.

But out of Lima, in El Campo—the country—where everybody is free as the air, everything is changed, everybody is happy, nothing goes wrong. The abundance is glorious, the ease and liberty delightful; there is nothing to equal it in the riding, dancing, eating, drinking, laughing, sleeping, dreaming, card-playing, smoking, joking world.

El Señor Paz Soldan, in his 'Historia del Peru Independiente,' says: 'Peru, essentially hospitable, admitted into her bosom from the first days of her independence thousands of foreigners, to whom she extended not only the same fellowship she afforded her own children, but such was the goodness of the country that she considered these new comers as illustrious personages. Men who in their native country had never been anything but domestic servants, or waiters in a restaurant, among whom there might perhaps be numbered one or two who, by their superior ability, might, after the lapse of twenty years, come to be master tailors or shopmen, have gained fortunes in Peru all at once, have won the hand of ladies of fortune, birth, riches, and social distinction. Those who have entered the army or navy have quickly risen to the highest posts. If they devote themselves to business, at once they become capitalists; and in civil and political appointments the foreigner is hardly to be distinguished from the native. The first decrees ever issued gave every protection and preference to foreigners resident in the country. They have the same right to the protection of the laws as Peruvians, without exception of persons, becoming of course bound by the same laws, to bear the same burdens, and in proportion to their fortunes to share in contributing to the income of the State. . . . Such as have any knowledge of science, or special industry, or are desirous of establishing houses of business, can reside in perfect freedom, and have given to them letters of citizenship. He who establishes a new industry, or invents a useful machine hitherto unknown in Peru, is exempt for a whole year from paying any taxes. If necessary, the Government will supply him with funds to carry on his art; and it will give free land to agriculturists. And yet, strange to say, and more painful to confess, many of these foreigners have been the cause of serious difficulties to the country, plunging it into conflicts which more or less have taken the gilt off the national honour. They have wished for themselves certain distinct national laws. They have thought themselves entitled to break whatever laws they pleased, and when the penalty has been enforced they have applied to their Governments, who have always judged the question in an aspect the most unfavourable to the honour and interest of Peru.'

As regards this hospitality given to English tailors and tailors' sons by Peru, it is quite true; true is it that they have married the rich daughters of ancient families, and made marvellous progress in all things that distinguished Dives from Lazarus. Men who would never have been anything but lackeys in their own country have become masters of lands and money in Peru. It is all true. Without wishing to disparage my own countrymen, and still less my countrywomen, I am bound to confess that the Peruvians have derived very little edification from their presence and example.

Within the Guano Age a British minister has been shot at his own table in Lima while dining with his mistress. The captain of an English man-of-war lying in Callao was murdered in the outskirts of Lima while on a drunken spree : the murderers in both cases never being brought to justice.

The English merchants were men noted for neither moral nor intellectual capacity, utterly innocent of any culture, or regard for it; of no manners or good customs that could reflect honour on the English name, and who gained fortunes after such fashion as only the practices of a corrupt government could sanction or connive at. Few English ladies have ever been permanently resident in Lima. It has been visited by one or two showy examples of the money-monger class; but the Lima people have not had the opportunity of knowing by actual contact in their own country the gentry of England. This has been a disadvantage to us and to them of the greatest magnitude : for while we have accepted the hospitality of Peru, we have not returned it in a manner worthy of the English name.

Nor can it be said that English travellers who have written on Peru make any very great figure in the cause of truth and honesty; whilst the amount of literary pilfering has been almost as notorious as that of the pillage of the public treasury by native officers of state.

The commanders and petty officers of the Steam Navigation Company in the Pacific come more in contact with the better class of Peruvians than any other portion of the English community. Among these numerous officers there are a few to be met with who can speak grammatical English. No doubt, grammar to a sailor is an irksome thing, at any rate it is a thing of minor importance, and we rather like our sailors to be free of everything except their courage, their gentleness, their love of truth, and, above all, their glorious self-abnegation. But it is a pitiable sight to see a British tar with lavender kid-gloves on his fists, Havannah cigars in his great mouth, widened by an early love for loud oaths, rings on his fingers, and other apings of the fine gentleman; and it is disgusting to see him dressed in an authority he knows not how to adorn, and placed in a position which he can only degrade. Yet these British tars are looked up to as English gentlemen, and, what is more, as English captains; and not a few Peruvians come to the natural conclusion that it is no great thing to be an English gentleman after all.

It is very grievous to make these remarks; justice demands, however, that if we would criticise the Peruvians from an English standpoint, we should take into consideration the English example which has been placed before them during all the years of an Age of Guano.

An English sailor in every part of the commercial world which he visits is too often a disgrace to himself and a dishonour to his country. But in Peru he is a standing disgrace to humanity. When on shore, if he is not drunk, he is kicking up a row. His language is foul, his manners brutal, his associates the off-scouring of the people, and his appearance that of a wild beast. We have of late been turning our attention to unseaworthy ships, and the amount of wise and unwise talk that this important subject has evoked has been great and surprising. It is a pity that no one has thought it necessary to take up the subject of the unworthy sailor, which should include not only the ignorant, drunken, and grossly depraved seaman, but the oftentimes illiterate, ill-conditioned, and brutal creature called a captain, who commands him.

There are many considerations why the captain of a British ship should be a man of good character, and there are imperative reasons why he should be compelled to earn a certificate of good conduct, as well as a certificate of proficiency in the science of navigation. The ability to represent the country whose flag he carries, as a man well-instructed and of good manners, is not the least of those reasons.

I recently had the opportunity of becoming personally acquainted with nearly five hundred captains of merchant ships in the Pacific. I am ashamed to confess that the French, the Italian, the North American, and the Swede were everyway superior men to the English captains. There were exceptions of course; the superiority was not in physical force, but in intelligence, in manners, in the cleanliness in which they lived, and the sobriety of their lives. If the Pabellon de Pica may be compared to a pig-stye, the British sailors who frequent its strand may be likened unto swine. Indeed, it is an insult to that filth-investigating but sober brute to compare him with a being who at certain times is at once a madman, a drunkard, and not infrequently a murderer. It is not easy to escape the conviction that captains such as these must be of use to their employers, and are needed for purposes for which ordinary criminals would be unfitted. At the Pabellon de Pica a choice selection of these British worthies may be seen daily getting drunk on smuggled beer, winding up with smuggled brandy, wallowing among the filthiest filth of that foul concourse of filthy inhuman beings, a detestable example to all who witness it; and a living ensample of what England now is to a guano-selling people.

All this has come of our trying to do some justice to the Peruvians, and no doubt it will become us as quickly as possible to attend to the mote which is in our own eye.

It should likewise be borne in mind that the Peruvians have suffered the greatest indignities at the hands of successive British Governments. Claims for money of the most vexatious, frivolous and irritating nature have been pressed upon Peru with an arrogance equal only to their ridiculous extravagance. When at last, with great difficulty, our Government has been induced to submit one of these claims to arbitration, judgment has invariably been given against us—as it only could, or ought to have been given.

This chapter should not be closed without noticing the fact that for nearly fifty years the English have had their own burying-place at Bella Vista, which is midway between Lima and Callao, and their own church and officiating chaplain. The Jews likewise have their synagogue, the Freemasons their lodges, the Chinese their temples; and although liberty of worship is not the law of the land, the utmost toleration in religious matters exists. The women of Lima, who have retained the old religion with ten times more firmness than the men, are the sole opponents of all religious reforms in the Peruvian Constitution. And because it is the women who stand in front of their Church, guarding it with their lives, let us have some respect for them. They are a powerful and determined body, as courageous as they are beautiful, which is saying much. In times of great excitement they will take part in the parliamentary debates! Not, indeed, in a parliamentary and constitutional manner, but in a manner quite effectual. These fair champions of their Church, when liberty of worship, or liberty of teaching, or any question that touches the Roman Catholic faith is being debated in the assembly, proceed thither in the tapada attire, with only one eye visible, and from the Ladies' Gallery will throw handfuls of grass to a speaker—intimating thereby his relationship to one of our domestic quadrupeds—or garlands of tinsel, just as it pleases them, and as the words of the speaker are for or against their cause. Our own House of Commons should take knowledge of this, and pause before they remove the lattice work from before their Ladies' Gallery!

## CHAPTER II.

The Mormons are coming to Peru. Five hundred families of this formidable sect are formally announced as being on their way to the land of the Incas, and the Peruvian Government has been very liberal in its grant of free land: this may be called a revolution indeed. A Spanish law existed in Peru but little more than half a century ago, which ran as follows: 'Because the inconveniences increase from foreigners passing to the Indies, who take up their residence in seaport towns and other places, some of whom are not to be trusted in the things of our holy Catholic faith, and because it becomes us diligently to see that no error is sown among the Indians and ignorant people, we command the Viceroys, the Audiencias, and the Governors, and we charge the Archbishops and Bishops that they do all that in them lies to sweep the earth of this people, and that they cast them out of the Indies and compel them to put to sea on the first occasion and at their own cost[1].' We may also note that among these sublime laws one may be found which absolutely forbade the importation of printed books.

Since then it cannot be denied that Peru has made great progress in the matter of toleration to foreigners. It has not perpetuated the insane and suicidal policy of the nation that expelled the Moors, the real bone and muscle of the country, from its soil. And it may truly be said that what the Moors were to Andalusia and Southern Spain,

---

[1] As early as 1614 we find Cervantes writing of these countries as the 'refugio y amparo de los desesperados de España, Yglesia de los alçados, salvoconducto de los homicidas, palay cubierta de los jugadores (á quien llaman ciertos los peritos en el arte) añagaza general de mugeres libres, engaño comun de muchos, y remedio particular de pocos'—or, in plain English, the Indies are the 'refuge and shield of the hopeless ones of Spain, the sanctuary of the fraudulent, the protection of the murderer, the occasion and pretext of gamesters (as certain experts in the art are called), the common snare of free women, the universal imposture of the many and the specific reparation of the few.'—*El Zeloso Estremeño*. In *La Española Inglesa* he calls the Indies 'el comun refugio de los pobres generosos,' he had himself sought service in the colonies, but anything in the form of favour from the Spanish court never fell to the lot of Cervantes. And all men of brave hearts and high courage may thank God that royal people were as powerless to spoil or to help men of genius then as they are still.

Europeans and Asiatics have been to Peru; supplying it not only with literature and science, but industry also. All the great estates of Peru are tilled by foreigners; so are its gardens. All the steam ships on its coast are driven by foreigners; foreigners surveyed and built their railways, their one pier, gave them gas, and would give them water if the Peruvian Government would only be wise. There is nothing of importance in the whole country that does not owe its existence to foreign capital and foreign thought, and it cannot be denied that Peru has done much in making her laws conform to such a state of things. It may yet do more. Ten more years of peace and tranquillity will work wonders in a land that at present may be said to be practically unacquainted with both. Ten years will close the accursed Age of Guano. Practically it may be said to be closed now. Peru is putting her house in order: she has learned much in the course of the last four years, and with economy, persisting in her present course of real hard, honest work, giving up playing at soldiers, and keeping an expensive navy which is of no earthly use to her, she may redeem herself from her past degradation, and become as great as she says she is.

But Mormons!

If there be a country in the teeming world which offers a field for Mormonism, it is Peru. If Mormonism be a belief that it is the chief end of man to multiply his species, to replenish the earth, and find the perfection of his being in subduing it, Peru is the very place for the Mormons. One might even go the length of saying that it was made on purpose for them.

Peru, with the immensity of its territory and the riches that are enclosed in it, requires a people with a religious faith in the divinity of polygamy and agriculture to make the most of the truly wonderful land.

Let the Mormons leave the country in which they are at present looked down upon, for one where they will be welcomed.

Mormonism is not, with the exception of its name, new to Peru. The Incas were great breeders of men, they pushed their humanising conquests north and south; not so much by the power of the spear and the sling, as by building great storehouses of maize. They first reduced the people whom they would conquer to the verge of starvation, and then fed them on sweeter food than they had ever tasted before. Count von Moltke was not the first who reduced a great city by besieging it, and surrounding it with a vast army. This was done in the days before the tragedy of Ollanta had been rehearsed in Cuzco. What the Incas gained by giving corn, they maintained by teaching the people how to grow and cultivate it. Men had as many wives as they pleased, provided that they were able to maintain them, and they had no fawning immoral priests to make women barren and unfruitful; who preached godliness to the people, but practised devilry themselves.

And here one may be allowed to notice by the way, that it is a thing altogether singular and inconsistent that these loud-tongued republicans and apostles of the rights of women, will allow and tolerate among them a body of men who believe that it is God's will they should burn and not marry, and cannot think of allowing among their mighty respectablenesses a people who believe that it is God's will they should have a plurality of wives. Perhaps when the great Americans are tired of the vanity of being a hundred years old, and can find time to look this matter in the face they may reconsider their Mormon policy, and give up persecuting a people who at least have many divine examples for their way of life. If Mormonism be good for South America, why should it not be good for the North? and what will be nothing less than the blessing of heaven on Lake Titicaca, why should it be esteemed a curse at the Lake of Salt? Happily the logic of great events in the lives of nations is more easy to comprehend than the logic of mere professors.

The history of colonisation in Peru is not interesting reading; much less so are the personal reports of those who have been connected with carrying out the various schemes of the Government. There were the usual delays, the usual difficulty in obtaining the promised funds at the appointed times, followed by confusion and disaster.

The first colony formed in Peru consisted of Germans, who established themselves at Pozuzo, a small district formed of mountains and valleys fifteen days journey north-east of Lima. The proposal was made in 1853, and the first batch of the new comers arrived in 1857. In 1870 they numbered 360 souls, 112 of whom were children. Their progress had not been very brilliant; among them were carpenters, coopers, cigar-makers, cabinet-makers, blacksmiths, shoe-makers, tailors, saddlers, machinists, and tanners. A priest, a grave-digger or clerk, a schoolmaster and an architect were also among the number. Each colonist was expected to cultivate a plot of ground measuring 33,000 yards by 13,000 yards, on which they grew tobacco, coca, maize, yuca (a most delicious farinaceous root), haricot beans, rice, coffee, and garden stuff. The people lived in wooden houses, and there were among them all three houses of wrought stone. An enthusiastic Peruvian deputy in giving a description of this little struggling colony, concluded his peroration thus: 'We have an eloquent example in the industrious colony established at Pozuzo, where in the midst of savage nature they have erected a city which perhaps is on a level with any city of Europe!' On which it might be remarked that there is a great deal of the perhaps, but very little of the city in this statement. It is in fact nothing but a city of the honourable deputy's brain.

The next emigration was from the islands of the South-western Pacific—subjects of his Majesty the King of Hawaii, whose diplomatic representative in Lima demanded the return of these people, who did return in an unexpected manner, to the earth out of which they were taken. They all died like flies that had been poisoned. The Peruvian Government then prohibited any further immigration of Polynesians.

.It was afterwards discovered that these people had been kidnapped, or, as the official report says, 'seduced first, and stolen afterwards.'

It had been eloquently preached by many ardent Peruvians, now that the subject of immigration for a moment or so seized hold of their warm brains, that all that was needed to fill Peru with happy colonists was to establish liberty of worship, toleration, a free press, dignity—moral and intellectual—security to persons and property, and when these great things were once placed on a firm basis in Peru the superfluous populations of the world would flock to the abundance it could offer, together with the warm and delightful sun, like doves to their windows. These things not having been done, the other has been left undone—albeit not for that specific reason. The immigrating class, for the most part, have their own way of procuring information regarding the country which courts their presence, and it is quite likely that the glad tidings from

Peru still require to be authenticated. Neither the Irish labourer, nor the Scotch, nor yet the Welsh have bestowed themselves on Peru, and it is to be hoped they never will until they can be sure of quick returns. The Cornish miner is well known in various localities for his drunkenness, his obstinacy, his cunning, and above all for his untruthfulness.

The Chinese immigration, if such it can be called, is the only considerable immigration that has ever taken place in Peru. It began as a commercial speculation; and there are many orthodox and highly respectable men in Lima who owe their wealth to the traffic in Chinese, in whose magnificent *salas* a conversation on China is as welcome as the mention of the gallows in a family, one of whose members had been hanged.

Of the 65,000 Chinese taken from their native land, 5,000 died on their way to Peru; they threw themselves overboard or smoked a little too much opium, or were shot, or all these causes were put together. It was once my lot to be seated in a very small room filled for the most part with guano men, where I was compelled to listen to the tale of an Italian who had served as chief mate on a ship freighted with Chinamen. He thought his life was once in danger.

'And what did you under the circumstances?' enquired some one.

'I shot two of them down, *sacramento*,' answered the villainous-looking wretch; on which there was a burst of laughter that did not seem to me very appropriate.

'And what was done with *you*?' I enquired in no sympathising tone.

'Senor,' replied the assassin, 'the Captain, Senor Venturini, accommodated me with a passage in his gig to the shore, where I remained to make an extended acquaintance with the Celestial Empire.'

The cold insolence of this criminal suggested to me that I had just as well keep my troublesome tongue as still as possible.

The Chinese question, as is natural that it should, has agitated the public mind in Lima not a little. At one time it assumed such alarming features that it was seriously proposed in Congress to expel the free Chinamen from Peru, or compel them to contract themselves anew[1]. It was known that the free

---

[1] See a useful work 'La Condicion Juridica de los Estrangeros en el Peru,' per Felix Cipriano C. Zegarra. Santiago, 1872. p. 136.

Chinamen stirred up their enslaved brethren to revolt; explained to them—which was perfectly true—that according to Peruvian law they could not be held in bondage, and if they escaped they could not be recaptured. Many attempts at escape were made and many murders were the result.

According to the Peruvian author quoted above, the Chinamen brought to the dung heaps of Peru, or its sugar plantations, are selected from the lowest of their race. 'The planters promote the natural degeneration of their Chinese labourers; they lodge them in filthy sheds without a single care being bestowed upon them, while they are condemned to a ceaseless unremitting toil, without a ray of hope that their condition will be ever bettered. For the enslaved Chinaman the day dawns with labour; labour pursues him through its weary hours, a labour which will bring no good fruit to him, and the shadows of night provide him with nothing but dreams of the tormenting routine which awaits him to-morrow. In his sickness he has no mother to attend him with her care; he has not even the melancholy comfort that he will be decently buried when he dies, much less that his grave will be watered with the sacred tears of those who loved him. Of the meanest Peruvian the authorities know where he lived, when he died, and for what cause, and where he is buried. But the Asiatics are disembarked and scattered among numerous private properties, their existence is forgotten, they do not live, rather they vegetate, and at last die like brutes beneath the scourge of their driver or the burden which was too heavy to bear. We only remember the Chinaman when, weary of being weary, and vexed with vexation, he arms himself with the dagger of desperation, wounds the air with the cry of rebellion, and covers our fields with desolation and blood.'

The great distance, observes the same author, of the private estates from the centre of authority, is one of the securities of their owners that their abuse of their Chinese slaves will neither be corrected or chastised. On the contrary, his influence with the local authorities is oftentimes such as to make them instruments of his designs. Between the master and the slave respect for the law does not exist, and the consequence is, that the one becomes more and more a despot, and the other more and more insolent and vicious.

Escape for the Chinaman is next to impossible;

he can only free himself from the horrible condition in which he finds himself by using his braces or his silken scarf for a halter, or the more quiet way of an overdose of opium.

Treat the Chinaman well, and he is a valuable servant, and happily many thousands of such are to be found along the coast, in several of the great haciendas, and in Lima. The wages of a Chinese slave are 4 dols. a month, two suits of clothes in the year, and his keep. A free Chinaman as a labourer earns a dollar a day, and of course 'finds' himself. Now and then one hears strange phrases at the most unexpected time, and one's ears tingle with words that an Englishman knows how to meet when compelled to hear them.

'How did you manage to do all that work?' was a question put at a dinner-table one night in Lima, when I was partaking of the awful hospitality of an English-speaking capitalist.

'Well,' was the reply, 'I bought half-a-dozen Chinamen, taught them the use of the machine, which the devils learned much quicker than I did, and in less than three months I found that I could easily make ten thousand dollars a month,' etc.

'I bought half-a-dozen Chinamen!' They might have been so many sacks of potatoes, or pieces of machinery, and the ease and familiarity with so repulsive a commerce which the speech denoted, proved too well the contempt which such familiarity always breeds.

The Chinaman is not only very intelligent, he is even superior in his personal tastes to many of those who pride themselves on being his masters. If he has time and opportunity he will keep himself scrupulously clean in his person and dress. After his day's work, if he has been digging dung for example, he will change his clothes and have a bath before eating his supper. He is polite and courteous, humorous and ingenious. He is by no means a coward, but will sell his life to avenge his honour. It is always dangerous for a man twice his size to strike a Chinaman. The only stand-up fight I ever saw in Lima, was between a small Chinaman and a big Peruvian of the Yellow breed; and the yellow-skinned 'big 'un' must have very much regretted the insult which originated the blows he received in his face from the little one. The Chinamen of the better class, the Wing Fats; Kwong, Tung, Tays; the Wing Sings; the Pow Wos; the Wing Hing Lees, and Si, Tu, Pous, whose acquaintance I made, are all shrewd, courteous, gentlemanlike fellows, temperate in all things, good-humoured and kind, industrious, and exquisitely clean in their houses and attire. It was an infinitely greater pleasure to me to pass an evening with some of these, than with my own brandy-drinking, tobacco-smoking, and complaining countrymen, whose conversation is garnished with unclean oaths, whose Spanish is a disgrace to their own country, and their English to that in which they reside.

My Chinese friends were greatly puzzled at the answer I gave to their questions why I had come to Peru, or for what purpose; they could not believe it, any more than they could believe that an English gentleman drank brandy for any other reason than that it was a religious observance.

'And why came you to Peru?' I enquired in my turn.

'To make money,' was the candid reply.

'For nothing else?' I insisted.

To give emphasis to his words Wing Hi rose from his seat, paced slowly up and down the room clapping his hands now behind his back, and now below his right knee: 'For nothing, nothing, nothing else,' he exclaimed, and laughed.

'Do you like Lima pretty well?' I enquired

with some care, for a Chinaman resents direct questions; and the answer invariably was—

'No. Lima is no good, there, is no money;' which many other shopkeepers not Chinamen can swear to, and their oaths in this instance are perfectly trustworthy.

'You do not give credit I suppose?' and I kept as solemn a face as possible in putting the question. My solemnity was speedily knocked out of me by the burst of boisterous laughter which greeted my question.

Wishing to cultivate these delightful heathens, I purchased from time to time a few things, all good, all very reasonable in price. These were chiefly fans, pictures, paper-knives, neckties, and boxes. Some of their ivory carving was a marvel of patience and keen sight. I was assured that one piece, for which they asked the price of 300 dols., took one man two years to make. That one statement made it an unpleasant object to behold. The porcelain brought to Lima is of the gaudiest and most inferior kind. I insisted on this so much that at last they confessed it to be true. 'But then the price,' they suggested.—A pair of vases that would sell in Bond Street for £150, can be purchased in Lima for less than £20.

One day I picked up a New Testament in Chinese, and after staying one evening with my celestial friends for an hour, I took it out of my pocket and asked them to be kind enough to read it for me, and tell me what it was about, for that in my youth my parents had not taught me that language and I was too old to learn it now. The next night our conversation was renewed, all being for the most part of the purest heathenism. They made no allusion to my New Testament; they evidently preferred to talk of other things, or to sell fans. At last in a tone of indifference I asked after my book, which one of their number produced out of a sweet-scented drawer.

'We do not know,' they said, 'what the book is about'; and therefore they could not tell me. They had read it? 'O yes; it was not a cookery book, nor a song book, nor a book about women; but seemed to be a pot of many things not well boiled.' There was no laughter, all was as serious as melancholy itself. I was a little disappointed, and came away without buying anything. It must require great gifts to be a missionary to the heathen, and especially the heathen Chinese. I should be inclined to think it to be as easy to bring a rich Chinaman to repentance as a rich Jew. The failure of my New Testament to make itself understood was a great blow to me. They might probably have understood some portions of the Book of Genesis better; but to my regret I had not the means of putting that to the test.

The mention of the Old Testament reminds me of a trivial incident which occurred one night in a magnificent sala in Lima, where were a good sprinkling of Spanish-speaking gentlemen and ladies, Italians and Germans, I being the only Englishman present. In course of the conversation it was demanded by some one, what were the two creatures first to leave the Ark: and it was at once answered by several voices 'the dove and the deer.' This appeared rather unsound to me, and I questioned the statement. So hot did the debate become, that it ended in a willing bet of £20, when after some difficulty a Bible was procured, and the dove and the raven won. The consternation was great. One man was candid enough to confess that he was an ass of no small magnitude for not reflecting that under the circumstances it could not well be a deer; but he had heard that such was the case, and because it was in the Bible felt bound to believe it.

Among all the classes of immigrants in Peru, or in Lima its capital, the English stand first and highest. They are certainly better represented than they were twenty years ago, but there is still much to improve. One great drawback to the English is the absence of a home, or the means of making one. The construction of the houses is one cause. There are no snug corners sacred to quiet and repose, and if the house be not a convent, it is something between a theatre and a furniture shop. Domestic servants are another fatal drawback, but the rent is the greatest of them all. The rents of some of the dingiest houses in the back streets are higher than those in Mayfair in the season, while the principal houses in the chief street are treble the amount. If I have elsewhere spoken sharply of my countrymen, it is because I think much of the land which gave them birth. It does not by any means follow that because a Peruvian child fifty years of age sells his soul to the devil, that an Englishman of four hundred should follow his example. It should be quite the other way.

The hotels are not, under the circumstances, unreasonable; a bachelor can live very well for thirty shillings a day, including fleas. Washing is a serious item in a city where there is much sun, much dust, little water, and the *lavendera* is the companion of 'gentlemen.'

New books are not remarkably dear, but the assortment is limited to theology and medicine. There are half-a-dozen daily newspapers, which cost half-a-crown a day if you buy them all. Their joint circulation will not reach more than fifteen thousand copies, while of their number only two may be said to pay their expenses; only one to make any profit. This is not to be wondered at. I tried my best to get into a controversy with them, by rousing them to jealousy. I publicly stated that if the guano deposits had been in Australia, or even in Canada, at a time when so much doubt was thrown on the quantity of guano they might contain, some newspaper would have sent off its special correspondent to make a report. The *Comercio*, the chief of the press, replied, with charming *naivete*: 'Why should we go to the expense of making a special report for ourselves when the Government will supply us with as many reports as we like?' The supply of English literature is very poor. Harper's Magazine appears to be in greatest demand, and certainly for the price of forty cents it is a marvel of cheapness. It is well printed, profusely and often well illustrated, and the numbers for the present year contain lengthy instalments of *Daniel Deronda*, and one or two original novels by American writers. There was not a single decent edition of the Don Quixote in any language to be found in all the shops of the city. There is evidently a brisk sale for very indecent photographs, and cheap editions of the Paul de Kock school. The number of new books printed in Lima is miserably small. The last, which has been very well received, is 'Tradiciones del Peru,' por Ricardo Palma, third series. It is exceedingly well written, and consists of a series of short stories illustrating the manners and customs of the early days. Here is one which for many reasons is worth doing into English. It is called 'A Law-suit against God,' and exhibits much of the old Spanish meal, and not a little of the new Peruvian leaven. It purports to be a chronicle of the time of the Viceroy, the Marquis de Castil-Dos-Rius.

In the archives of what was once the Real Audiencia de Lima, will be found the copy of a lawsuit once demanded by the King of Spain, which covers more than four hundred folios of stamped paper, from which with great patience we have been able to gather the following—

## I.

GOD made the good man: but it would seem that His Divine Majesty threw aces when He created mankind.

Man instinctively inclines to good, but deceit poisons his soul and makes him an egotist, that is to say, perverse.

Whosoever would aspire to a large harvest of evils, let him begin by sowing benefactions.

Such is humanity, and very right was the King Don Alonso the Wise, when he said—'If this world was not badly made, at least it appeared to be so.'

Don Pedro Campos de Ayala was, somewhere about the year 1695, a rich Spanish merchant, living in the neighbourhood of Lima, on whom misfortunes poured like hail on a heath.

Generous to a fault, there was no wretchedness he did not alleviate with his money, no unfortunate he did not run to console. And this without fatuity, and solely for the pleasure he had in doing good.

But the loss of a ship on its way from Cadiz with a valuable cargo, and the failure of some scoundrels for whom Don Pedro had been bound, reduced him to great straits. Our honourable Spaniard sold off all he possessed, at great loss, paid his creditors, and remained without a farthing.

With the last copper fled his last friend. He wished to go to work again, and applied to many whom, in the days of his opulence, he had helped, and solely to whom they were indebted for what they had, to give him some employment.

Then it was he discovered how much truth is contained in the proverb which says '*There are no friends but God, and a crown in the pocket.*'

Even by the woman whom he had loved, and in whose love he believed like a child, it was very clearly revealed to him that now times had indeed changed.

Then did Don Pedro swear an oath, that he would again become rich, even though to make his fortune he should have recourse to crime.

The chicanery of others had slain in his soul all that was great, noble, and generous; and there was awakened within him a profound disgust for human nature. Like the Roman tyrant, he could have wished that humanity had a head that he might get it on to a block; there would then be a little chopping.

He disappeared from Lima, and went to settle in Potosi.

A few days before his disappearance, there was found dead in his bed a Biscayan usurer. Some said that he had died of congestion, and others declared that he had been violently strangled with a pocket handkerchief.

Had there been a robbery or the taking of revenge? The public voice decided for the latter.

But no one conceived the lie that this event coincided with the sudden flight of our Protagonist.

And the years ran on, and there came that of 1706, when Don Pedro returned to Lima with half a million gained in Potosi.

But he was no longer the same man, self-denying and generous, as all had once known him.

Enclosed in his egotism, like the turtle in his shell, he rejoiced that all Lima knew that he was again rich; but they likewise knew that he refused to give even a grain of rice to St. Peter's cock.

As for the rest, Don Pedro, so merry and communicative before, became changed into a misanthrope. He walked alone, he never returned a salutation, he visited no one save a well-known Jesuit, with whom he would remain hours together in secret converse.

All at once it became rumoured that Campos de Ayala had called a notary, made his will, and left all his immense fortune to the College of St. Paul.

But did he repent him of this, or was it that some new matter weighed heavily on his soul? At any rate, a month later he revoked his former will and made another, in which he distributed his fortune in equal proportions among the various convents and monasteries of Lima; setting apart a whole capital for masses for his soul, making a few handsome legacies, and among them one in favour of a nephew of the Biscayan of long ago.

Those were the times when, as a contemporary writer very graphically says, 'the Jesuit and the Friar scratched under the pillows of the dying to get possession of a will.'

Not many days passed after that revocation, when one night the Viceroy, the Marquis de Castil-dos-Rius, received a long anonymous letter which, after reading and re-reading, made his excellency cogitate, and the result of his cogitation was to send for a magistrate whom he charged without loss of time with the apprehension of Don Pedro Campos de Ayala, whom he was to lodge in the prison of the court.

## II.

Don Manuel Omms de Santa Pau Olim de Sentmanat y de Lanuza, Grandee of Spain and Marquis de Castil-dos-Rius, was ambassador in Paris when happened the death of Charles II, and which involved the monarchy in a bloody war of succession. The Marquis not only presented to Louis XIV the will in which the Bewitched one carried the crown to the Duke of Anjou, but openly declared himself a partisan of the Bourbon, and also procured that his relatives commenced hostilities against the Archduke of Austria. In one of the battles, the firstborn of the Marquis de Castil-dos-Rius died.

It is well known that the American Colonies accepted the will of Charles II acknowledging Philip V as their legitimate sovereign. He, after the termination of the civil war, hastened to reward the services of Castil-dos-Rius, and he named him Viceroy of Peru.

Señor de Sentmanat y de Lanuza arrived in Lima in 1706, and it could not be said that he governed well when he began to raise his loans and impose taxes on private fortunes, religious houses, and capitular bodies: but by this means he was able to replenish the exhausted treasury of his king with a million and a half of crowns.

Among the most notable events of the time in which he governed may be reckoned the victory which the pirate Wagner gained over the squadron of the Count de Casa-Alegre, thereby doing the English out of five millions of silver travellers from Peru. This animated the other corsairs of that nation, Dampier and Rogers, who took possession of Guayaquil, and squeezed out of that municipality a pretty fat contribution. In trying to restrain these marauders, the Viceroy spent a hundred and fifty thousand dollars in fitting out various ships, which sailed from Callao under the command of Admiral Don Pablo Alzamora. Everybody was anxious for the fray, even to the students of the colleges, all burning to chastise the heretics. Fortunately, the fight was never begun, and when our fleet went in search of the pirates as far as the Galapagos islands, they had abandoned already the waters of the Pacific.

The earthquake which ruined many towns in the province of Paruro was also among the great events of the same period.

Among the religious occurrences worthy of mention were the translation of the nuns of Santa Rosa to their own convent, and the fierce meeting in the Augustine chapter-room between the two Fathers, Zavala the Biscayan, and Paz the Sevillian. The Royal Audiencia was compelled to imprison the whole chapter, thereby suppressing the greatest of disorders, and after a session of eighteen hours and a good deal of scrutiny Zavala triumphed by a majority of two votes.

The venerable Marquis de Castil-dos-Rius was an enthusiastic cultivator of the muses; but as these ladies are almost always shy with old men, a very poor inspiration animates the few verses of his excellency with which we happen to have any knowledge.

Every Monday the Viceroy had a reunion of the poets of Lima in the palace; and in the library of the chief cosmographer, Don Eduardo Carrasco, there existed until within a few years a bulky manuscript, *The Flower of the Aca-*

*demies of Lima*, in which were guarded the acts of the sessions and the verses of the bards. We have made the most searching investigations for the hidingplace of this very curious book, fatally without any result, which we suppose to be in possession of some avaricious bookworm, who can make no use of it himself, nor will allow others to explore so rich a treasure.

The little Parnassus of the palace, which after the manner of Apollo was presided over by the Viceroy, was formed of Don Pedro de Peralta, then quite a youth; the Jesuit José Buendia, a Limeño of great talent, and prodigious science; Don Luis Oviedo y Herrera, also a Limeño, and son of the poet Count de la Granja (author of a pretty poem on Santa Rosa); and other geniuses whose names are not worth the trouble of recording.

It was during the festivities held in honour of the birth of the Infanta Don Luis Fernando, that the little Parnassus was in the height of its glory, and the Viceroy, the Marquis de Castildos-Rius, gave a representation at the palace of the tragedy of Perseus, written in unhappy hendecasyllables, to judge by a fragment which we once read. The principal of the clergy and aristocracy assisted at the representation.

Speaking of the performance, our compatriot Peralta, in one of the notes to his *Lima fundada*, says, that it was given with harmonious music, splendid dresses, and beautiful decorations; and that in it the Viceroy not only manifested the elegance of his poetic genius, but also the greatness of his soul and the jealousy of his love.

It appears to us that there is a good deal of the courtier in that criticism.

Castil-dos-Rius had hardly been two years in his government before they accused him to Philip V of having used his high office for improper purposes, and defrauded the royal treasury in connivance with the *contrabandistas*. The Royal Audiencia and the Tribunal of Commerce supported the accusation, and the Monarch resolved upon at once dismissing the Governor of Peru from his office; but the order was revoked, because a daughter of the Marquis, one of the Queen's maids of honour, threw herself at the feet of Philip V, and brought to his recollection the great services of her father during the war of succession.

But although the King appeased the Marquis in a way by revoking the first order, the pride of Señor de Olim de Sentmanat was deeply wounded; so much so that it carried him to his tomb, April 22nd, 1710, after having governed Peru three years and a half.

The funeral was celebrated with slight pomp, but with abundance of good and bad verses, the Little Parnassus fulfilled a duty towards their brother in Apollo.

### III.

The anonymous letter accused Don Pedro Campos de Ayala of assassinating the Biscayan, and stealing a thousand ounces, which served for the basis of the great fortune he acquired in Potosi.

What proofs did the informer supply? We are unable to say.

Don Pedro being duly installed in the Stone Jug, the Mayor appeared to take his declaration; and the accused replied as follows:

'Mr. Mayor, I plead not guilty when he who accuses me is God himself. Only to Him under the seal of confession did I reveal my crime. Your worship will of course represent human justice in the case against me, but I shall institute a suit against GOD.'

As will be seen, the distinctions of the culprit

were somewhat casuistical, but he found an advocate (the marvel would have been had he not) prepared to undertake the case against God. Forensic resource is mighty prolific.

For the reason that the Royal Council sought to wrap the case in the deepest mystery, all its details were devoured with avidity, and it became the greatest scandal of the time.

The Inquisition, which was hand and glove with the Jesuits, sought diligently for opportunities, and resolved to have a finger in the pie.

The Archbishop, the Viceroy, and the most ingrained aristocrat of Lima society took the side of the Company of Jesus. Although the accused sustained his integrity, he presented no other proof than his own word, that a Jesuit was the author of the anonymous denunciation and the revealer of the secret of the confessional, instigated thereto by the revocation of the will.

On his part the nephew of the Biscayan claimed the fortune of the murderer of his uncle, while the trustees of the various hospitals and convents defended the validity of the second will.

All the sucking lawyers spent their Latin in the case, and the air was filled with strange notions and extravagant opinions.

Meanwhile the scandal spread; nor will we

venture to say to what lengths it might have gone, had not His Majesty Don Philip V declared that it would be for the public convenience, and the decorum of the Church as well as for the morality of his dominions, that the case should be heard before his great Council of the Indies in Spain.

The consequence was that Don Pedro Campos de Ayala marched to Spain under orders, in company with the voluminous case.

And as was natural, there followed with him not a few of those who were favourably mentioned in the will, and who went to Court to look after their rights.

Peace was re-established in our City of Kings, and the Inquisition had its attention and time distracted by making preparation to burn Madam Castro, and the statue and bones of the Jesuit Ulloa.

What was the sentence, or the turn which the sagacious Philip V gave to the case? We do not know; but we are allowed to suppose that the King hit upon some conciliatory expedient which brought peace to all the litigants, and it is possible that the culprit ate a little blessed bread, or shared in some royal indulgence

Does the original case still exist in Spain? It is very likely that it has been eaten of moths, and hence the pretext and origin of a phrase which with us has become so popular.

It is said of a certain notary who much troubled the Royal Council in the matter of a will and its codicils, that when the custodian of such things at last produced something which looked like the original, he said, 'Here it is, but the moths have sadly eaten it.'

'Just our luck, my dear sir,' said an interested one, who was none other than the Marquis of Castelfuerte. And ever since, when a thing has disappeared we say 'No doubt the moths have eaten it.'

So much for the lawsuit against GOD, which only a Spaniard could have conceived and a Peruvian satirist report.

When a commercial father sees his eldest son, on whom he has lavished much care and money that he might learn mathematics and such an amount of classics as will stand him in good stead at the fashionable training grounds of the world's gladiators, and the boy is seen to forsake figures and take to poetry, to prefer the gay science to that which would enable him to master the money article of the *Times*, that father will feel as great a pang as when a giant dies.

The same feeling may actuate many a Peruvian bondholder when he is told that the Peruvians are beginning to cultivate literature. Many city men will disregard the thing altogether, or disdain to take notice of it. Many will treat it with resentment and contempt. What right have people who are in debt to busy themselves in writing books, in amusing themselves when they should be at work, and in writing poetry when they should be making money. And yet the cultivation of literature for its own sake by any people ought not only to be viewed with favour, it should be carefully watched, to see if it be a real national growth or only a momentary effort which cannot last. If it be the former, we shall see it in an improvement of public morals and manners; in the quickening of the national conscience and chastening the public taste, in an elevation of character and in fresh dignity being imparted to the common things and duties of everyday life.

Peru possesses a history as well as a country. The one remains to be written, and the other to be described by a Peruvian genius who shall do for Peru and Peruvian history what Sir Walter Scott did for his native land and its records.

It is now high time that Peru produced her popular historian. One who can fire the intellect of his countrymen while he provides them with an elevating pastime, who can point out the way they should or should not go by showing them the ways they have hitherto travelled. If the work has been delayed, it is because the people have too long retained the spirit of the former times to make it possible for them to profit by any explanation of the past. Monarchists yet, because they have never known better, they have not been taught to hate the hateful kings who ruled them in selfishness and kept them in ignorance, while they have not learned to love with devotion and intelligence the freedom they possess but know not how to use.

When books are found in hands till then only accustomed to carry muskets, and the pen is handled by those who have hitherto only believed in the power of the sword, we may rest assured that an important change has set in, a silent revolution has begun, which will make all other revolutions very difficult if not impossible.

## CHAPTER III.

WHETHER it be true, or only a poetical way of putting it, that Yarmouth was built on red herrings, Manchester on cotton, Birmingham on brass, Middlesborough on pigs of iron, and the holy Roman Catholic Church in China on Peruvian bark, it is true that the Government of Peru has for more than a generation subsisted on guano, and the foundations of its greatness have been foundations of the same[1];—the ordure of birds—pelicans, penguins, boobies, and gulls

---

[1] Since writing the above I have come on the following passage from the report of the Peruvian Minister of Finance for 1858.

'HUANO

Tan grande es el valor de este ramo de la riqueza nacional, que sin exajeracion puede asegurarse, que en su estimacion y buen manejo estriba la subsistencia del Estado, el mantenimiento de su credito, el porvenir de su engrandecimiento, y la consérvacion del órden publico.' Which may be done into the vulgar tongue faithfully and well as follows—So great is the value of this branch of the national riches, that without exaggeration it may be affirmed that on its estimation and good handling depend the subsistence of the State, the maintenance of its credit, the future of its increase, and the preservation of public order.—Signed, Manuel Ortiz de Zerallos.

of many kinds, and many kinds of ducks, all of marine habits, and deriving their living solely from the sea and the sky which is stretched above it.

This precious Guano, or Huano, according to the orthography of the sixteenth century, had long been in use in Peru before Peru was discovered by the Spaniards. It was well enough known to those famous agriculturists, the Incas, who five centuries ago used it as a servant. With the change which changed the Incas from off the face of the earth, came the strangest change of all,—Guano ceased to be the servant or helper of the native soil; it became the master of the people who occupy it, the Peruvian people, the Spanish Peruvians who call themselves Republicans.

No disgrace or ignominy need have come upon Peru for selling its guano and getting drunk on the proceeds, if it had not trampled its own soil into sand, and killed not only the corn, the trees, and flowers which grow upon it, but also the men who cultivate those beautiful and necessary things [1].

---

[1] It is hard to believe that the present dead silent sands, which form the coast of Peru from the Province of Chincha in the south as far as Trujillo in the north, was in the early days so populous

During the time that Peru has been a vendor of guano, it has sold twenty million tons of it, and as the price has ranged from £12 to £12 10s. and £13 the ton, Peru may be said to have turned a pretty penny by the transaction. What she has done with the money is a very pertinent question, which will be answered in its right place.

The amount of guano still remaining in the country amounts to between seven and eight million tons. There are men of intelligence even in Peru who affirm that the quantity does not reach five million tons. One of my informants, a man intimately connected with the export and sale of this guano, assured me that there are not at this hour more than two million tons in the whole of the Republic, and he had the best possible means at his disposal for ascertaining its truth. I have since discovered,

---

that Padre Melendez, quoted by Unanue, compared one of the small valleys to an ant hill; and now 'not more than half a dozen natives can be found among its ruins.'—See Documentos Literarios del Peru Colectados por Manuel de Odriozola, vol. vi, p. 1,79.

The rapid and continued decrease of the Peruvian population has been ascribed to civil war. This is not true. Where the sword has carried off its thousands, the infernal stuff known as brandy, the small pox, and other epidemics, have slain their tens of thousands. The liberation of the slaves also caused great mortality amongst the negroes.

however, that men who deal in guano do not always speak with a strict regard for the truth.

As this is one of the vexed questions of the hour to some of my countrymen, the violent lenders of money, Jews, Greeks, infidels and others; although I have no sympathy with them, yet on condition that they buy this book I will give them a fair account of the guano which I have actually seen, and where it exists.

I was sent to Peru for the express purpose of making this examination. I may therefore expect that my statements will be received with some consideration. They have certainly been prepared with much care, and, I may add, under very favourable circumstances.

My visits to the existing guano deposits were made after they had been uncovered of the stones which had been rolled upon them by the turbulent action of a century of earthquakes, the sand which the unresisted winds of heaven for the same period had heaped upon them from the mainland, and the slower but no less degrading influences of a tropical sun, attended with the ever humid air, dense mists, fogs and exhalations, and now and then copious showers of rain. Moreover, my visits were made after a certain ascertained quantity of guano had been removed, and my measurements of the quantity remaining were therefore easily checked.

Last year the Pabellon de Pica was reported to contain eight million tons of guano. At that time it was covered from head to foot with more than fifty feet of sand and stones. The principal slopes are now uncovered. Before this painful and expensive process had been completed, various other courageous guesses had been made, and the Government engineers were divided among themselves in their estimates. One enthusiastic group of these loyal measurers contended for five million tons, another for three million five hundred and twenty thousand six hundred and forty, and another, unofficial and disinterested, placed it at less than a million tons.

My own measurements corroborate this latter calculation. There may be one million tons of guano on the Pabellon de Pica. The exact quantity will only be known after all the guano has been entirely removed and weighed.

The Pabellon de Pica is in form like a pavilion, or tent, or better still, a sugar-loaf rising a little more than 1000 feet above the sea which washes its base. It is connected by a short saddle with the mountain range, which runs north and south along the whole Peruvian coast, attaining a height here of more than 5000 feet in isolated cones, but maintaining an average altitude of 3000 feet.

When a strong north wind rages on these sandy pampas, the dust, finer than Irish blackguard, obscures the sky, disfigures the earth, and makes mad the unhappy traveller who happens to be caught in its fury. A mind not troubled by the low price of Peruvian bonds, or whether even the next coupon will be paid, might imagine that the gods, in mercy to the idleness of man, were determined to cover up those dunghills from human sight; and hence the floods, and cataracts of sand and dust which have been poured upon them from above.

If it could be conceived that an almighty hand, consisting of nineteen fingers, each finger six hundred feet long, with a generous palm fifteen hundred feet wide, had thrust itself up from below, through this loaf of sugar, or dry dung, to where the dung reaches on the Pabellon, some idea might be formed of the frame in which, and on which the guano rests.

The man who reckoned the Pabellon to contain eight million tons of guano, took no notice of the Cyclopean fingers which hold it together, or the winstone palm in which it rests. There are eighteen large and small gorges formed by the nineteen stone fingers. Each gorge was filled with a motionless torrent of stones and sand, and these had to be removed before the guano could be touched.

So hard and compact had the guano become, that neither the stones nor the sand had mixed with it; when these were put in motion and conducted down into the sea below, the guano was found hard and intact, and it had to be blasted with gunpowder to convey it by the wooden shoots to the ships' launches that were dancing to receive it underneath. The process was as dangerous as mining, and quite as expensive, to the Peruvian Government; for, although the loading of the guano is let out by contract, the contractors—a limited company of native capitalists—will, as a matter of course, claim a considerable sum for removing stones and sand, and equally as a matter of course they will be paid: and they deserve to be paid. No hell has ever been conceived by the Hebrew, the Irish, the Italian, or even the Scotch mind for appeasing the anger and satisfying the vengeance of their awful gods, that can be equalled in the fierceness of its heat, the horror of its stink, and the damnation of those compelled to labour there, to a deposit of Peruvian guano when being shovelled into ships. The Chinese who have gone through it, and had the delightful opportunity of helping themselves to a sufficiency of opium to carry them back to their homes, as some believed, or to heaven, as fondly hoped others, must have had a superior idea of the Almighty, than have any of the money-making nations mentioned above, who still cling to an immortality of fire and brimstone.

Years ago the Pabellon de Pica was resorted to for its guano by a people, whoever they were, who had some fear of God before their eyes. Their little houses built of boulders and mortar, still stand, and so does their little church, built after the same fashion, but better, and raised from the earth on three tiers, each tier set back a foot's length from the other. It is now used as a store for barley and other valuable necessaries for the mules and horses of the loading company.

If the bondholders of Peru, or others, have any desire to know something of public life on this now celebrated dunghill, they may turn to another page of this history, and Mr. Plimsoll, or other shipping reformer, may learn something likewise of the lives of English seamen passed during a period of eight months in the neighbourhood of a Peruvian guano heap. In the meantime we are dealing with the grave subject of measurable quantities of stuff, which fetches £12 or so a ton in the various markets of the cultivated world.

The next deposit—of much greater dimensions, although not so well known—is about eight miles south of the Pabellon, called Punta de Lobos. This also is on the mainland, but juts out to the west considerably, into the sea. I find it mentioned in Dampier—'At Lobos de la Mar,' he says, vol. i. 146, 'we found abundance of penguins, and boobies, and seal in great abundance.' Also in vol. iv. 178 he says, 'from Tucames to Yancque is twelve leagues, from which place they carry clay to lay in the valleys of Arica and Sama. And here live some few Indian people, who are continually digging this clayey ground for the use aforesaid, for the Spaniards reckon that it fattens the ground.' The fishing no doubt was better here than at the Pabellon, which would be the principal attraction to the Indians. The Indians have disappeared with the lobos, the penguins and the boobies.

One million six hundred thousand tons of guana were reported from Lobos last year by the Government engineers. The place is much more easy of access than the Pabellon, and no obstacle was in the way of a thorough measurement, and yet the utmost carelessness has been observed with regard to it. It may safely be taken that there are two millions and a half of tons at this deposit, or series of deposits, ten in number, all overlooking the sea. The guano is good. If the method of shipping it were equally good the Government might save the large amount which they at present lose. I have no hesitation in saying, that for every 900 tons shipped, 200 tons of guano are lost in the sea by bad management, added to the dangers of the heavy surf which rolls in under the shoots. As at the Pabellon de Pica, so here the principal labourers are Chinamen, and Chilenos, the former doing much more work than the latter, and receiving inferior pay. Many of the Chinamen are still apprentices, or 'slaves' as they are in reality called and treated by their owners.

At Punto de Lobos I discovered two small

caves built of boulders, and roofed in with rafters of whales' ribs. The effect of the white concentric circles in the sombre light of these alcoves had an oriental expression. The number of whales on this coast must at one time have been very great. They are still to be met with several hundred miles west, in the latitude of Payta. No doubt for the same reason that the lobos and the boobies have gone, no one knows where, so the whales have gone in search of grounds and waters remote from the haunts of man and steamers.

A singular effect of light upon the bright slopes of dazzling sand which run down from the northern sides of the Point, was observed from the heights: when the shadows of the clouds in the zenith passed over the shining surface they appeared to be not shadows, but last night's clouds which had fallen from the sky, so dense were they, dark, and sharply defined. [It frequently happens in Peru, that what appears to be substantial, is nothing better than a morning cloud which passes away.]

Huanillos is another deposit still further south, where the guano is good but the facilities for shipping it are few. Here are five different gorges, in which the dung has been stored as if by careful hands. The earthquake however has played sad havoc with the storing. From a great height above, enormous pieces of rock of more than a thousand tons each have been hurled down, and in one place another motionless cataract of heavy boulders covers up a large amount of guano.

The quantity found here may be fairly estimated at eight hundred thousand tons.

It was easy to count ninety-five ships resting below on what, at the distance of three miles, appeared to be a sea without motion or ripple. At the Pabellon de Pica there were ninety-one ships, and at Lobos one hundred and fourteen ships, all waiting for guano: three hundred ships in all, some of which had been waiting for more than eight months; and it is not unlikely that the whole of them may have to wait for the same length of time. An impression has got abroad that the reason of this delay is the absence of guano. It is a natural inference for the captain of a ship to draw, and it is just the kind of information an ignorant man would send home to his employers. It is however absolutely erroneous; the delays in loading are vexatious in the extreme, but being in Peru they can hardly be avoided. Their cause may be set down to the sea and its dangers, the precipitous rocky shore, the ill-constructed launches and shoots, and now and then to the ignorance, stupidity, and obstinacy of a Peruvian official, called an *administrador*.

Chipana, six miles further south of Huanillos, is another considerable deposit. But as this had not been uncovered, and the place is absolutely uninhabited and without any of the common necessaries of life, which in Peru may be said to be not very few, I did not visit it, and am content to take the measurement of a gentleman whom I have every reason to trust, and on whose accuracy and ability I can rely as I have had to rely before.

The amount of guano at Chipana may be taken at about the same as Huanillos. If to this be added the deposits of Chomache, very small, Islotas de Pajaros, Quebrada de Pica, Patache, and all other points further north, up to la Bahia de la Independencia, we may safely declare that among them all will be found not less than five million tons of good guano.

Before proceeding to give an account of the deposits in the north, it may be well to allude to a question of considerable importance to some one, be it the Government of Peru, or the house of Messrs. Dreyfus Brothers, the present financial agents of Peru. The only interest which the question can have for the public, or the holders of Peruvian bonds, arises from the fact of this question involving no less a sum than £1,500,000 or even more; and if the Government of Peru has to pay it, so much the worse will it be for its already alarmed and disappointed creditors. Many of the three hundred ships lying off the three principal deposits of the South, have been there for very long periods of time, and a considerable bill for demurrage has been contracted. The question is who is to pay the shipowners' claim, and probably the law courts will have to answer the question. It would appear at first sight that this charge should be paid by Dreyfus. According to the first article of the contract between that firm and the Government of Peru, Dreyfus was to purchase two million tons of guano, and to pay for the same two million four hundred thousand pounds sterling. Here is a distinct act of purchase. The guano is the property of Dreyfus. The second article of the contract would appear to provide especially for the case in point: 'Los compradores enviarán por su cuenta y riesgo, á los depositos huaneros de la Republica, los buques necesarios para el transporte del huano' [the purchasers shall send, *at their own cost and risk*, the necessary ships to the guano deposits of the Republic for the purpose of transporting the guano].

This would seem to be plain enough: but these ships, or the greater part of them, came chartered by Dreyfus, not to any deposit of guano, in the first instance, but to Callao, where they collected in that bay, notorious now for many reported acts of singular heroism, and other acts of a very different nature. The ships were finally detained by command of the President of the Republic, who, acting on certain subterranean knowledge, refused to despatch the ships, or to allow them to proceed to the deposits. Dreyfus, the President insisted, had already taken away all the guano that belonged to them, and therefore the ships which they had chartered for carrying away still more should not be allowed to go and load. At last the President appears to have discovered his mistake, and the ships, to the amazement of the Lima press, were allowed to depart; some to the Pabellon de Pica, where they still are;

others to Lobos, and the rest to Huanillos. In the meantime the following circular appeared.

'The Lima press has commented in various articles on the conduct of our house with respect to the export of guano, and we have been charged with endeavouring to appropriate a larger quantity than that which is stipulated in our contracts as sufficient to cover the amounts due to us by the Supreme Government.

These false and malevolent assertions render it necessary for us to satisfy the public and inform the country of the state of our affairs with the Supreme Government.

We trust that dispassionate people who do not allow their opinions to be based on partial evidence, will do our house the justice to which we are entitled by these few particulars, the truth of which is proved by facts and figures that can be authenticated by application to the offices of the Public Treasury.

| | | |
|---|---:|---:|
| Balance in favour of our house on June 30, 1875, as per account delivered, embracing 1,377,150 tons of guano | | $.24,068,156 |
| Expenses since that date for monthly instalments, loading, salaries in Europe, etc. | | $.2,390,000 |
| Balance in favour of our house | | $.26,459,156 |
| From this sum there is to be deducted the value of cargoes despatched up to June, 300,092 tons at 30 soles | 9,002,760 | |
| Vessels now loading, 394,966 tons at 30 soles | 4,849,000 | |
| * Vessels detained in Callao 110,657 tons at 30 soles | 3,319,710 | |
| | | $.24,181,470 |
| Which shews a balance in our favour of | | $.2,286,686 |
| Adding to this sum interest in account current since June | 1,500,000 | |
| † Cost of loading ships at the deposits and in Callao | 1,500,000 | |
| | | 3,000,000 |
| Shewing a clear balance in our favour of | | $.5,286,686 |

We have taken thirty soles as the average value of guano of different qualities.

These figures prove that our house not only has not received more than it is entitled to, even if all the vessels had left which are at the deposits as well as those in Callao, but that there is still a heavy balance due to us.

With respect to questions now pending, no one possesses the right to consider his opinions of more value than those of the tribunals of justice before which they now are, without the least opposition on our part.

DREYFUS, HERMANOS, & Co.

*Lima, Dec.* 31, 1875.

It appears from this statement *, that Dreyfus had already put in their claim for the detention of the ships. What is meant by the last item marked with a † is uncertain; no ships are loaded in Callao. If the Government can sustain its suit against Dreyfus on that part of the second article of the contract mentioned above, instead of its owing Dreyfus the 'clear balance of 5,286,686 dols.' Dreyfus is in debt to the Government.

But there is another item in the second article which appears to override the first: viz. 'y este (guano) será colocado por cuenta y riesgo del gobierno abordo de las lanches destinadas a la carga de dichos buques' [or, in plain English, 'this guano shall be placed on board such launches as are appointed to carry it to the ships, on account and at the risk of the Government'].

Well, it is absolutely certain that the guano was not *colocado*, or placed on board the appointed launches; not because the launches were not there; not because there was no guano at the deposits;—but simply because the Government had not, for some reason or other, fulfilled its own part of the contract.

No answer was made by the Government to Dreyfus' circular, and the obsequious Lima newspapers were as silent upon it as dumb dogs. I have since heard, on high authority, that the reply of the Government is prepared, and that it disputes Dreyfus' claims and will contest them in a court of law.

I was glad when they said unto me, let us go to the islands of the north; glad to leave behind me the filthiness, foulness, and weariness of the mainland in the neighbourhood of the Pabellon de Pica. Had it not been for the true British kindness of one or two of my countrymen and several Americans in command of guano ships, Her Majesty's Consular agent, and the agent of the house of Dreyfus, who did all they could to provide me with wholesome food, German beer, and clean beds, I should have fled away from that much-talked-of dunghill without estimating its contents; or like a philosophical Chinaman sought out a quiet nook in the warm rocks, and with an opium reed in my lips smoked myself away to everlasting bliss.

On my return from the south we passed close to the Chincha islands. When I first saw them twenty years ago, they were bold, brown heads, tall, and erect, standing out of the sea like living things, reflecting the light of heaven, or forming soft and tender shadows of the tropical sun on a blue sea. Now these same islands looked like creatures whose heads had been cut off, or like vast sarcophagi, like anything in short that reminds one of death and the grave.

In ages which have no record these islands were the home of millions of happy birds, the resort of a hundred times more millions of fishes, of sea lions, and other creatures whose names are not so common; the marine residence, in fact, of innumerable creatures predestined from the creation of the world to lay up a store of wealth for the British farmer, and a store of quite another sort for an immaculate Republican government. One passage of the

Hebrew Scriptures, and this the only passage in the whole range of sacred or profane literature, supplies an adequate epitaph for the Chincha islands. But it is too indecent, however amusing it may be, to quote.

On Sunday morning, March 26th, of the last year of grace, I first caught sight of the beautiful pearl-gray islands of Lobos de Afuera, undulating in latitude S. 6.57.20, longitude 80.41.50, beneath a blue sky, and apparently rolling out of an equally blue sea. Here is the only large deposit that has remained untouched; here you may walk about among great birds busy hatching eggs, look a great sea-lion in the face without making him afraid, and dip your hat in the sea and bring up more little fishes than you can eat for breakfast.

There are eight distinct deposits in an island rather more than a mile in length and half a mile in width. The amount of guano will be not less than 650,000 tons.

It is not all of the same good quality, for considerable rain has at one time fallen on these islands. Wide and deep beds of sand mark in a well defined manner the courses of several once strong and rapid streams. But if the poor guano, that namely which does not yield more than two per cent. of ammonia be reckoned, the deposits on these islands will reach a million tons.

The wiseacres who believe guano to be a mineral substance, and not the excreta of birds, will do well to pay a visit to Lobos de Afuera. There they will see the whole process of guano making and storing carried on with the greatest activity, regularity, and despatch. The birds make their nests quite close together: as close and regular, in fact, as wash-hand basins laid out in a row for sale in a market-place; are about the same size, and stand as high from the ground. These nests are made by the joint efforts of the male and female birds; for there is no moss, or lichen, or grass, or twig, or weed, available, or within a hundred miles and more: even the sea does not yield a leaf. As a rule, about one hundred and fifty nests form a farm. It has been computed by a close observer that the heguiro will contribute from 4 oz. to 6 oz. per day of nesty material, the pelican twice as much. When there are millions of these active beings living in undisturbed retirement, with abundance of appropriate food within reach, it does not require a very vivid imagination to realise in how, comparatively, short a time a great deposit of guano can be stored.

Will the Government of Peru occupy itself in preserving and cultivating these busy birds? That Government has lived now on their produce for more than thirty years; why should it not take a benign and intelligent interest in the creatures who have continued its existence and contributed to its fame?

The heguiro is a large bird of the gull and booby species, but twice the size of these, with blue stockings and also blue shoes. It does not appear to possess much natural intelligence, and its education has evidently been left uncared for. It will defend its young with real courage, but will fly from its nest and its one or two eggs on the least alarm. This, however, is not always the case. But in a most insane manner if it spies a white umbrella approaching, it sets up a painful shriek. Had it kept its mouth shut, the umbrella had travelled in another direction. As the noise came from a peculiar cave-like aperture in the high rocks, I sat down in front, watched the movements of the bird, who kept up a dismal noise, evidently resenting my intrusion on her private affairs. After a brief space I marched slowly up to the bird, who, when she saw me determined to come on, deliberately rose from her nest, and became engaged in some frantic effort, the meaning of which I could not guess. When I approached within ten yards of her, she sprang into the sky and began sailing above my head, trying by every means in her power to scare me away. When I reached the nest, I found the beautiful pale blue egg covered with little fishes! The anxious mother had emptied her stomach in order to protect the fruit of her body from discovery or outrage, or to keep it warm while she paid a visit to her mansion in the skies.

Birds have ever been a source of joy to me from the time that I first remember walking in a field of buttercups in Mid Staffordshire, some fifty years ago, and hearing for the first time the rapturous music of a lark. Since then I have watched the movements of the great condor on the Andes, the eagle on the Hurons, the ibis on the Nile, the native companion in its quiet nooks on the Murray, the laughing jackass in the Bush of Australia, the curaçoa of Central America, the tapa culo of the South American desert, the albatross of the South Pacific. I can see them all still, or their ghosts, whenever I choose to shut my eyes, a process which the poets assure us is necessary if we would see bright colours. And now I no longer care for birds. I have seen them in double millions at a time, swarming in the sky, like insects on a leaf, or vermin in a Spanish bed. They are as common as man, and can be as useful, and become as great a commercial speculation as he.

We visited the island of Macabi, lat. 7.49.30 S., long. 79.28.30, for the purpose of seeing what good thing remained there that was worth removing in the way of houses, tanks and tools for use on the virgin deposits of Lobos de Afuera. Although there is not more than one shipload of guano left, I was glad to see the place for many reasons. It will be recollected that it was on the guano said to exist on this and the Guañapi islands that the Peruvian Loan of 1872 was raised, and it will be the duty of all who invested their money in that transaction to enquire into the truth of the statements on which the loan was made.

Macabi is an island split in two, spanned by a very well constructed iron suspension bridge a hundred feet long. The birds which had been frightened away by the operations of the guano-loading company have returned. The lobos probably never left the place, the precipitous rocks and the great caverns which the sea has scooped out affording them sufficient protection from the 'fun'-pursuing Peruvian, who delights in killing, where there is no danger, an animal twice his own size, and whose existence is quite as important as his own. Or if the lobos did leave, they also have returned. This would go to prove the statements that the birds have begun to return to the Chinchas. When this is proved beyond any doubt, we may expect to hear of Messrs. Schweiser and Gnat applying for another loan on the strength of the pelicans, ducks and boobies having returned to their ancient labours on those celebrated islands.

The spectacle presented at Macabi was humiliating. The ground was everywhere strewn with Government property, which had all gone to destruction. The shovels and picks were scattered about as if they had been thrown down with curses which had blasted them. I went to pick up a shovel, but it fell to pieces like Rip Van Winkle's gun on the Catskills; the wheelbarrows collapsed with a touch. Suddenly I came on a little coffin, exquisitely made, not quite eighteen inches long. There it lay in the midst of the burning glaring rocks, as solitary and striking as the print of a foot in the sand was to Robinson Crusoe. The coffin was empty, and the presence of certain filthy-fat gallinazos high up on the rocks explained the reason. A little further on were the graves of some fifty full-grown persons, 'Asiatics,' probably, who had purposely fallen asleep. Walking down the steady slope of the island till I came to the edge of the sea, which rolled below me some hundred and twenty feet, I came suddenly in front of a thousand lobos, all basking in the sun after their morning's bath. It was a sight certainly new, entertaining, and instructive. The young lobos are silly little things, and look as if it had not taken much trouble to make them; a child could carve a baby lobo out of a log, that would be quite as good to look at as one of these. But the old fathers, patriarchs, kings, or presidents of the herd, are as impressive as some of Layard's Assyrian lions. Suddenly one of these caught me in his eye, and no doubt imagining me to be a Peruvian, signalled to the rest, who, following his lead, all rushed violently down the steep place into the sea, and began tumbling about and rolling over in the surf like a mob of happy children gambolling among a lot of hay-cocks in a green field. They live on fish, and the number of fishes is as great at Macabi as elsewhere. As I remained watching these swarthy creatures, a great sea-lion appeared above the surface of the rolling deep looking about him, his mouth full of fishes, just as you have seen a high-bred horse with his mouth full of straggling hay, turn his head to look as you entered his stable door.

My next and longer visit was to Lobos de Tierra, lat. S. 6.27.30, the largest guano island in the world, being some seven miles long, or more. Here are great deposits of guano, the extent and value of which are not yet known. It is certain that there are more than eight hundred thousand tons of good quality in the numerous deposits which have been hitherto examined.

On January 31st, being in lat. S. 7.50.0, and some 15 miles from the Peruvian coast, when on my way to the South from Panama, we ran into a heavy shower of rain. Now it is much more likely to rain in lat. S. 6.27.30 and 120 miles from the shore, and this explains the reason why the guano deposits of Lobos de Tierra were not worked before. Still the quantity of rich material found there is great, and it is the only place where I came on sal ammoniac *in situ*; the crystals were large and beautifully formed, but somewhat opaque. During the ten days I remained there, more than 500 tons of good guano were shipped in one day, and there were some 40 ships waiting to receive more.

Like all the other guano deposits, Lobos de Tierra has to be supplied at great expense from the mainland with everything for the support of human life. It is true that the sea supplies very good fish, but man cannot live on fish alone, at least for any length of time, especially if he is engaged in loading ships with guano. The Changos, however, a race of fishermen on the Peruvian coast, do live on uncooked fish, and a finer race to look at may not be found; the colour of their skin is simply beautiful, but they are very little children in understanding. It is only fair to say that with their raw fish they consume a plentiful amount of chicha, a fermented liquor made from maize, the ancient beer of Peru: and very good liquor it is, very sustaining, and, taken in excess, as intoxicating as that of the immortal Bass. These hardy fishers visit all these islands in their balsas, great rafts formed of three tiers of large trees of light wood, stripped and prepared for the purpose in Guayaquil. They are precisely the same as those first met with by Pizarro's expedition when on his way to conquer Peru, three centuries and a half ago. The people are probably the same, except that they now speak Spanish, and are never found with gold; but now and then they do traffic in fine cottons, spun by hand, now as then, by natives of the country.

I cannot forget that it was at Lobos de Tierra I had the great pleasure of forming the acquaintance of one who represents young Peru: the new generation that, if time and opportunity be given it, may transform that land of corruption into a new nation. Here on this barren island, I found a son of one of the oldest Peruvian families, thoroughly educated, well acquainted with England and its literature, proud of his country, jealous for its honour, and keenly alive to the disgrace into which she has been dragged by the wicked men who have gone to their doom. Should this generation, represented by one whom I am allowed to call my friend—who, though born in the Guano Age is not of it,—rise into power, the rising generation in England may see what many have had too great reason to despair of, namely, a South American Republic, that shall prefer death to dishonour, and if needs must, will live on bread and onions in order to be free of debt. There is so much pleasure in hoping the best of all men, that it surely must be a duty the neglect of which, when there are substantial evidences to support it, must be a crime.

I left Lobos de Tierra with profound regret, but it was necessary to do so in order to see what remained to be seen of the precious dung in other parts of Peru. The following will be found to be a fair approximation of the quantities existing along the northern coast.

| Islands. | Latitude. | Longitude. | Quantities. Tons. |
|---|---|---|---|
| Malabrigo | 7.43.20 | 79.26.20 | 400 |
| Macabi | 7.49.30 | 79.28.20 | 1,000 |
| Guañapi | 7.49.30 | 78.56.0 | 3,500 |
| Chao | 8.46.50 | 78.46.0 | 800 |
| Coreobado | 8.57.0 | 78.40.30 | 3,000 |
| Santa | 9.03.0 | 78.39.30 | 100 |
| Bay of Ferrol | 9.10.0 | 78.36.0 | 22,000 |
| El Dorado | 9.12.0 | 78.34.0 | 6,000 |
| Small Island Pajarros | 9.12.0 | 78.30.10 | 250 |
| Tortuga | 9.21.30 | 78.27.0 | 700 |
| Mongon | 9.39.40 | 78.25.0 | 23,000 |
| Mongon 2nd | 9.40.0 | 78.20.0 | 30,000 |
| Mongoncillo | 9.45.30 | 78.16.40 | 6,000 |
| Cornejos | 9.53.0 | 78.15.0 | 500 |
| Erizos | 9.54.40 | 78.14.0 | 5,000 |
| Huarmey | 10.00.20 | 78.12.0 | 500 |
| 2nd ditto | 10.02.0 | 78.11.0 | 3,000 |
| Bay of Gramadal | 10.25.0 | 78.00.30 | 10,000 |
| Pescadores | 11.48.0 | 77.15.30 | 200 |

I have not visited all these small deposits, and have been content to take the report of Captain Black, the chief of the Peruvian expedition lately appointed to examine them. I have found him so faithful and trustworthy in those cases—the more important of them all—where I have had the opportunity of comparing his calculations with my own, that I have not hesitated to adopt his estimates of the least important deposits. I have considered them of value if for no other reason than to guard the public against any fresh discovery being made by interested parties.

If then we add these northern deposits to those of the south, Peru has at present in her possession, in round numbers, 7,500,000 tons of guano of 2240 lbs. to the ton.

It is not my business to suggest the possible existence of guano remaining to be discovered. I may however be allowed to say that there are certain unmistakable indications of even large deposits which may lie buried a hundred feet below the sand on the slopes of the southern shore. As those indications are the result of my own observation, I may be allowed to keep them to myself for a more convenient season.

## CHAPTER IV.

'However long the guano deposits may last, Peru always possesses the nitrate deposits of Tarapaca to replace them. Foreseeing the possibility of the former becoming exhausted, the Goverment has adopted measures by which it may secure a new source of income, in order that on the termination of the guano the Republic may be able to continue to meet the obligations it is under to its foreign creditors.'

These words form part of an assuring despatch from Don Juan Ignacio Elguera, the Peruvian Minister of Finance, to the Minister of Foreign Affairs, and was made public as early as possible after it was found that the January coupon could not be paid. The assurance came too late for any practical purposes, and it merely demonstrated the fact that the Peruvian Government shared in the panic which had been designedly brought to pass by its enemies as well as its intimate friends in Lima, and their emissaries in London and Paris.

The despatch demonstrates two or three other matters of importance. We are made to infer from its terms, and the eagerness with which it insists on the undoubted source of wealth the Government possesses in the deposits of nitrate, that it was unaware of the actual amount of guano still remaining in the deposits of the north and the south. We may also safely believe that the Peruvian Government did not at the time of the publication of the despatch, dream of asking the bondholders to sacrifice any of their rights; and further, in its anxiety to save its credit with England, it was hurried into a confession which it now regrets.

What spirit of evil suggested to President Pardo the idea of appealing to the charity of his creditors, immediately after allowing his finance minister to announce to all the world that the Republic was able to continue meeting its obligations to its foreign creditors even though the guano should give out, it does not much concern us to enquire. The effect of such an appeal cannot fail to be prejudicial to the credit of Peru; and men or dealers in other people's money will not be wanting who will call in question the good faith of the finance minister when he declared that the deposits of nitrate could continue what the deposits of guano had begun but failed to carry on.

Other considerations press themselves upon us. In the midst of the crisis, the President published a decree, announcing that he would avail himself of the resolution of Congress which enabled him to acquire the nitrate works in the province of Tarapaca. A commission of lawyers was at once despatched to the province to examine titles, and to fix upon the price to be paid to each manufacturer for his plant and his nitrate lands. In an incredibly short time no less than fifty-one nitrate makers had given in their consent to sell their works to the Government, and the price was fixed upon each, and each was measured, inventoried, and closed. The total sum to be paid for these establisments was 18,000,000 dols. But they remained to be conveyed. The civil power had displayed considerable activity; now that the law had to be applied things became as dull as lead, and as heavy as if they had all been made of that well-known metal. Negotiations had also to be entered into with the Lima Banks, which is an operation as delicate and as dangerous as negotiating with so many volcanoes, or any other uncertain and baseless institutions of which either nature or a civilisation supported by bits of paper can boast.

Still the world was comforted by the promise that next week all would be well, or the week after, or say the end of the month, in order to be sure. In the midst of this, General Prado, the possible future President of Peru, is despatched to Europe on a mission, the nature of which was kept a profound secret for three weeks.

Simple men, who believed in the despatch of the finance minister, knew for certain that General Prado had gone to England to raise more money on nitrate, in order that the Oroya Railway might be finished, and a station-house built somewhere in the Milky Way, which it is destined probably this marvellous line shall ultimately reach. And if London would only lend Peru, say another £10,000,000, then Lima would rejoice, and the whole earth be glad; the mountains would break out into psalms, and the valleys would laugh and sing, for would not Don Enrique Meiggs, the Messiah[1] of the Andes, once more return to reign?

At any rate it is quite certain that General Prado was announced to sail on the 14th of March, when the last stroke of the pen was to be put to the conveyance of the nitrate properties. Alas! the law's delay continued, and General Prado did not sail. It is natural to suppose at all events that Prado never meant to go to London without the nitrate contracts in his pocket—which will supply a larger income to Peru than the guano in all its glory ever did,—for the purpose of asking the bondholders to be merciful. The General finally left Callao for Europe on the 21st, amidst the forebodings of his friends, and the ill-concealed joy of his foes, but without the nitrate documents being signed. Still, before he could reach London the thing would be done, and the result could be telegraphed. In the meantime the new minister to Paris and London, Rivaguero, telegraphed to Lima some favourable news, the precise terms

---

[1] 'Haber aparecido en el Peru el hombre que sin profanacion de la palabra se puede llamar el *Mesias* de los ferrocarriles para la salvacion de la Republica Peruana.'—El Ferrocarril de Arequipa, Historia, &c., Lima, 1871, p. lxxxi.

of which, of course, were not allowed to transpire, to the effect that an arrangement had been made satisfactory to all parties.

On this, further delay takes place in the important nitrate negotiations, and that in the face of a semi-official communication to the effect that next week merchants might rely upon it that all would be well and truly finished. In the stead of this, President Pardo 'reminds the Banks of an item which up to that period had never been dreamed or thought of, except by the President himself, namely, that they, the Banks, on the security of the nitrate bonds, would have to supply to the Government so many hundred thousand dollars per month!

All at once the whole fabric of the nitrate business fell down.

Two things may be inferred from this: President Pardo hoped, believed, perhaps knew, that the bondholders would give way, and he had become convinced that he had made a mistake in buying the nitrate properties; it is also likely that he knew for certain at this time that there was guano enough for all purposes, without meddling with the important nitrate matters, and thereby destroying a great and important national industry. He may also have been desirous to bury, in an oblivion of his own making, the honest compromise contained in the despatch of Don Juan Ignacio Elguera. A further light may have dawned on the Presidential mind, namely, that it will be perfectly easy for the Goverment to treble the export duty on nitrate, without in the least damaging the trade or dangerously interfering with the profits of the makers, by which means the Peruvian Government would reap an annual income without trouble, or any of the thousand vexations to which it has been subjected in the export and sale of its guano.

That it was the original intention of the Government to raise a loan on the 'purchase' of the nitrate properties, is evident from the terms of the tenth article of President Pardo's decree, which may be thus translated:—

'The establishments sold to the State shall be paid for within two years, or as soon after as possible, that funds for the purpose have been raised in Europe; payment shall be by bills on London, at not more than ninety days, and at the rate of exchange of forty-four pence to the *sol*,' etc.

Whatever value these particulars may possess

or have given to them by future events [1], they will serve to show some of the peculiar features of the Peruvian Government, and to what shifts it can resort, or is compelled to make under adverse circumstances, or circumstances into which it may be brought by its enemies, or its own weakness, its inherent lack of stout-hearted honesty, and its inaptitude for what is known as business.

The nitrate deposits are well enough known. It is absolutely certain that in the year 1863 there were sold 1,508,000 cwts.; and in 1873 5,830,000 cwts. In that year the Government acknowledged to have received from the export of this article the sum of 2,250,000 dols. Should the permanent sale of nitrate reach 5,000,000 quintals per annum, there is no reason why the Government should not realise from this source at least 10,000,000 dols. a year: should it only double its present duties the amount would reach 12,000,000 dols.

The annual amount of nitrate which the fifty-one establishments proposed to be bought by the Government are capable of producing, may be set down at 14,000,000 cwts.

These establishments do not exhaust the

[1] Written off Alta Villa, April 25, 1876.

whole of the nitrate deposits. There are several large 'Oficinas,' as they are called, which have, for their own reasons, refused to sell their properties to the State.

The region of these deposits is a wild, barren pampa, 3000 feet above the level of the sea, and contains not less than 150 square miles of land, which will yield on the safest calculation more than 70,000,000 tons of nitrate.

Why these establishments for the manufacture of this important substance are called 'oficinas' it may not be difficult to say: it is doubtless for the same reason that a cottage *orné* at Chorrillos, the Brighton of Lima, is called a rancho. Twenty years ago Chorrillos was to Lima what the Clyde and its neighbouring waters were to the manufacturing capital of Scotland. What Dunoon and its competitors on the Scotch coast now are, such has Chorrillos become,—the fashionable resort of rich people who have robbed nature of her simplicity and beauty by embellishing her, as they call it, with art. All that remains of the straw-thatched rancho of Chorrillos, with its unglazed windows, its mud floors, its hammocks, and its freedom, is its name. An oficina twenty or thirty years ago, was no doubt a mere office made of wood, hammered together hastily, as an extemporary protection from the sun by day, and the cold dews and airs of the night: in appearance resembling nothing else but an Australian outhouse. An oficina of to-day is a very different thing. Its appearance, and all that pertains to it, is as difficult to describe as a great ironworks, or chemical works, or any other works where the ramifications are not only numerous, but novel. The first oficina whose acquaintance I had the honour and trouble to make, was that of the Tarapaca Nitrate Company, situated near the terminus of the Iquique and La Noria Railway, in the midst of a windy plain 3000 feet above the sea, and beneath a far hotter sun than that which beats on the pyramids of Egypt.

If you take a seat in the wide balcony of the house, where the manager and the clerks of the establishment reside, and live not uncomfortably, you look down almost at your feet on what appears to be an uncountable number of vast iron tanks containing coloured liquids, a tall chimney, a chemical laboratory, an iodine extracting house, a steam-pump, innumerable connecting pipes, stretching and twisting about the vast premises as if they were the bowels of some scientifically formed stomach of vast proportions for the purpose of digesting poisons and producing the elements of gunpowder, a blacksmith's forge, an iron foundry, a lathe shop, complicated scaffolding, tramways, men making boilers, men attending on waggons, bending iron plates, stoking fires, breaking up *caliche*, wheeling out refuse, putting nitrate into sacks, and other miscellaneous labour, requiring great intelligence to direct and great endurance to carry on; and all beneath the fierce heat of a sun, unscreened by trees or clouds, the glare of which on the white substance which is in process of being turned over, broken, and carried from one point to another, is as painful as looking into a blast furnace. Beyond the great and busy area where all these varied operations are carried on the eye stretches across a desert of brown earth, which is terminated by soft rolling hills of the same fast colour. The appearance of this desert is that of a vast number of ant-hills in shape; and in size of the heaps of refuse which give character to the Black Country in Mid Staffordshire. Perhaps the first impression which this repulsive desert makes on the mind of a man who has seen and observed much is that of a battlefield of barbarian armies, where the slain still lie in the heaps in which they were clubbed down by their foes; or it may be likened to an illimitable number of dust-hills jumbled together by an earthquake. All this is the result of digging for *caliche*, and blasting it out of the sandy bed in which it has lain God only knows how long.

As the breeze springs up, and clouds of fine white dust follow the mule carts and rise under the hoofs of galloping horses, the idea of the battlefield with the use of gun-powder comes back on the memory, and is perhaps the nearest simile that can be used. And this is an oficina! one of the silliest and most inadequate of words ever used to denote what is one of the newest, and may be the largest, as it is certainly the most novel, of all modern industrial establishments.

The manufacture of caliche into nitrate of soda is not without its dangers to human life, though these are fewer than they were when men frequently fell into vats of boiling liquors, or broke their limbs in falling from high scaffolding: the latter form of danger still exists, and is almost impossible to guard against. I am free to say, however, that if the guard were possible I do not believe it would be used. There are some trades and processes which not only brutalise the labourers on whom rests the toil of carrying them on, but which no less degrade the mind of those who direct them; and the nitrate manufacture is one of these. 'Joe,' one of the house dogs, fell into one of the heated tanks of the oficina where I was staying, and his quick but dreadful death made more impression on some than did the untimely death of a man who was killed the day before at the same place. Another item in the agitated landscape which stretches from the balcony where I sat is a spacious burying-ground, walled in as a protection from dogs and carts; but these are not its only or its chief desecrators. The sky furnishes many more. This great oficina contains 1682 estacas; can produce 900,000 quintals of nitrate a year, and was 'sold' to the Government for 1,250,000 dols.

An estaca is a certain amount of ground 'staked out,' as we might say, and contains about one hundred square yards of available land.

There are other oficinas of still greater value than the one mentioned above; as, for instance, those of Gildemeister and Co., and which the Government acquired on the same terms for the same sum.

The markets for this new substance are England, Germany, the United States, California, Chile, and other countries. It is as a cultivator a formidable competitor of the guano, and is esteemed by scientific men to be much more valuable. Its price is set down at £19 the ton, although £12 and £12 10s. is its present market value. The acquisition by the Peruvian Government of this industry was patriotic, even if it were not wise. It was done with the intention of paying the foreign creditors of the Republic. Since then Peruvian patriotism has assumed another form and complexion, and what was done in an honest enthusiasm of haste is already being repented of in a leisure largely occupied with the contemplation of a patriotic repudiation of national duty and debt.

The arguments by which 'prominent' Peruvians are fortifying themselves for a step which at any moment may be taken, are neither moral nor convincing, except to themselves. 'Peru must live,' they say, which does not mean a noble form of poverty, but an altogether ignoble form of extravagance, and even wasteful magnificence. We must have our army, our navy, our President, his ministers, our judges, our priests, our ambassadors, our newspapers, stationery, bunting, gas for the plaza on feast days, wax candles for our churches by night and by day, a national police, gunpowder, jails for foreign delinquents, and railways to the Milky Way, to show to neighbouring republics and all the world that Peru is a fine nation.

There is not one of all these splendid items which, so far as the people are concerned, could not be dispensed with.

But to live, they reiterate, is the primary object and purpose of all nations, and especially republican nations, forgetting, or, what is much more likely, never having known, that death is preferable to a shamed life, and that there are times when it is clearly a duty to die.

The next argument now rapidly gaining ground in Lima is that although the guano has been hypothecated, this was contrary to Peruvian law, which distinctly lays down that nothing movable *can* be hypothecated; and as guano is clearly movable stuff, which can be proved to the meanest capacity—the capacity, namely, of a holder of Peruvian bonds—the

Government has been breaking its own laws for a generation past, and it is now time that this illegal conduct should cease. This is backed up by reminding all men, and especially Peruvians, who will derive great comfort from it, that England having recognised the primary fact that it is the first duty of a man to live, has abolished imprisonment for debt in her own dominions, and therefore she could not exert her power to make Peru pay what she owes, if Peru officially declares that she is unable to do so. These and other like arguments are being openly discussed in the Peruvian capital. Another, and perhaps the most formidable of all these specious pleas is, that England has recently let off Turkey, and therefore there is no reason why she should not let off Peru.

It is only fair to say that there are a few thoughtful men in the City of Kings who, ambitious for their country's honour, would fain see some arrangement made that will enable Peru to pursue her present policy of internal improvement, and help these men, who for the most part are very wealthy, to remain peaceably in office for say ten years longer—or say six—but at least, for God's sake as well as your own, they appealingly persist, let it not be less than four years (in the which there shall be no hearing or harvest for bondholders and dupes of that stamp).

There is no doubt that, in the words of 'a Daniel say I,' if the bondholders would not lose all, 'then must the Jew be merciful,' let them insist on their pound of flesh, and everything denominated in their bond, they will share the fate of Shylock. The only part of that cruel rascal's fate which they need have no apprehension of sharing is, being made into Christians.

It is unquestionably to be feared that if the present Government, and the one that succeeded it in August last under the presidency of General Prado, cannot defend the country from revolt, great disaster will follow not only to the republic, but most certainly to the bondholders.

Revolt is not only possible, it is expected. An armed force led by determined men from without, aided by traitors within, and backed by unscrupulous persons who would be willing to risk one million pounds sterling on the chance of making two millions, might easily—or if not easily, yet with pains—bring back the corrupt days of Balta and Castilla, and, with shame be it said, such people can find a precedent for their proposed scheme in houses of high standing, the heads of which are doubtless looked upon as irreproachable ensamples of cultivated respectability.

[Since writing the above, General Prado has once more assumed supreme power in peace, but there have followed two attempts at revolution within the space of three little months.]

## CHAPTER V.

HAVING set forth two principal sources of Peruvian income, let us now proceed to a third. When los Señores Althaus and Rosas appeared in Paris last autumn as the representatives of the Government of Peru, among other national securities which those gentlemen offered for a further loan of money, were the railways of Peru. They are six in number, only one of which is finished according to the original contracts. The amount of mileage however is considerable, so also may be said to be their cost, for the Government has paid to one contractor alone no less a sum than one hundred and thirty millions of dollars. There are other railways whose united lengths amount to about 150 miles; with one exception they cost little, and without an exception they all bring in much.

These do not belong to the Government. The Government railways cost enormous sums and bring in nothing; and it may safely be said that they will never figure, honestly, in the national accounts, except as items of expenditure. The Government of the day would only be too glad to become cheap carriers of the national produce, if there were any produce ready to carry. But the Government built their railways without considering what are the primary and elementary use of railways. It is incredible, but none the less true, that the Peruvians believing the mercantile 'progress' of the United States to spring from railways, thought that nothing more was needed to raise their country to the pinnacle of commercial magnificence than to build a few of these iron ways, and have magic horses fed with fire to caper along them; especially if they could get an American—a real go-a-head American—for their builder. And they did so.

The railway fever has had its virulent type in all parts of the world where railways have appeared. In Peru from 1868 to 1871-2 this fever was perhaps more active and deadly than anywhere; than in Canada, even, which is saying much, for there it took the form of a religious delirium. The Peruvians believed that if they offered a great and wonderful railway to the deities of industry, great and happy commercial times would follow. Just as they believe that give a priest a pyx, a spoon, some wine, and wheaten bread, he can make the body and blood of God; so they believed that give a great American the required elements, he could by some equally mysterious power make Peru one of the great nations of the earth.

Mr. Henry Meiggs [1], of Catskill 'city' in New York State, was on this occasion selected as the great high-priest who was to perform the required wonders. Give this magician a few thousand miles of iron rails to form two parallel lines, and a steam engine to run along them, and the vile body of the Peruvian Republic should be changed into a glorious body [2] with a mighty palpitating soul inside of it; the body to be of the true John Bull type for fatness, and the Yankee breed for speed.

---

[1] For the biography of this estimable gentleman see 'El Ferrocarril de Arequipa Historia, documentada de su origen construcion é inauguracion.'—Lima, p. 96. 'Ese hombre era ENRIQUE MEIGGS, cuyo nombre va unido inseparable é imperecederamente á los trabajos mas colosales de las republicas del mar Pacifico.'

[2] For these and similar ebullitions of profanity I am indebted to the Lima newspapers of the period, and one or two anonymous pamphlets.

This new meaning of the doctrine of transubstantiation was preached to willing and enchanted ears. Ten thousand labourers of all colours and kinds were introduced into the country. 'By God, Sir, there was not a steamboat on the broad waters of the Pacific that did not pour into Peru as many peones as potatoes from Chile.' These ten thousand men all went up the Andes bearing shovels in their hands, and singing the name of Meiggs as they went. Millions of nails, and hammers innumerable, rails and barrows, sleepers and picks, chains, and double patent layers, wheels and pistons, with many thousand kegs of blasting powder 'let in duty free,' with all the other infernal implements and apparatus for making the most notable railway of this age[1], poured into Peru marked with the name of Meiggs. You could no more breathe without Meiggs, than you could eat your dinner without swallowing dust, sleep without the sting of fleas or the soothing trumpet of musquitoes. Meiggs everywhere; in sunshine and in storm, on the sea and on the heights of the world, now called Mount Meiggs; in the earthquake[2], and in the

---

[1] Paz-Soldan.
[2] With a liberality on a scale equal to all his achievements, Mr.

peaceful atmosphere of the most elegant society in the world. The wonderful activity on the Mollendo and Arequipa railway, carried on without ceasing, produced an ecstasy of hope, and also an eruption of blasphemy. Every valley was to be exalted; every Peruvian mountain, hitherto sacred to snow and the traditions of the Incas, should be laid low by the wand of Meiggs; the desert of course should blossom as the rose: no more iron should be sharpened into swords; ploughshares and pruning-hooks should be in such demand, that every blade and dagger or weapon of war in the old world would be required to make them. And a highway should be there, in which should be no lion, even a highway for our GOD. All this mixture of trumpery metaphors were poured into the ears of the enchanted Peruvians for the space of three years and more. The railway as far as Arequipa was at length finished, the Oroya railway was begun.

It will probably never be finished.

Robert Stephenson is reported to have said once before a Railway Committee: 'My Lords and Gentlemen, you can carry a railway to the

---

Meiggs subscribed $50,000 for the sufferers in the terrible earthquake which desolated Arequipa and destroyed Arica in 1868.

Antipodes if you wish; it is only a matter of expense.' The Peruvians, aided by the arch-priest Meiggs, 'the Messiah of railways, who was to bring salvation to the Peruvian Republic,' and steadfastly believing in the Meiggs' method of transubstantiation, commenced building a railway, not to Calcutta, but to the moon [1].

[1] It is difficult to be original in this age of metaphor. Only this morning, April 26, and quite by accident, I came on a little print which is published, I believe, in Callao, where I found the following:

'RAILROADS IN THE CLOUDS.

'Looking over our exchanges we found the following. It is from the New York *Sun* of January 16, and gives an account of Mr. John G. Meiggs being "interviewed" in that city.

'Mr. John Meiggs, brother of Henry Meiggs, the "King of Peru," as the millionaire contractor is called in South America, is lodging in the Clarendon Hotel. He is a tall, large man, past middle age, and with a clear penetrating hazel eye. He has an important share in the management of his brother's affairs. "Peru," he said, "is richer in the precious metals than any other country in the world. Our engineers in building the railroad from the coast to Puno have come across a hundred silver mines, any one of which might be profitably worked, if in the United States. If these mines are worked, the railroads we have built will be a blessing to the country."

'Reporter—"I understand that there are marvels of engineering on some of your railroads?"

'Mr. Meiggs—"Yes. One of our roads crosses the mountains at 16,000 feet above the level of the sea. Some of the bridges, too, are very lofty, and built with a skill that would do credit to any part of the world."

'Reporter—"Your brother is said to be worth several millions of dollars?"

As early as 1859 the Oroya Railway began to be thought of seriously, and the late President of Peru, with two other gentlemen of character, were appointed a commission to collect data and make calculations for a railway between Lima and Jauja. Nothing, however, was done until 1864, when Congress authorised the Government, Castilla then being President, to construct a railway to Caxamarca, with an annual guarantee of 7 per cent. for twenty-five years.

The railway fever now began to increase in force and virulence, and in 1868 the President of the Republic was authorised to construct railways from Mollendo to Arequipa, Puno and Cuzco; from Chimbote to Santa or Huaraz; from Trujillo to Pacasmayo and to Caxamarca; from Lima to Jauja; and others which the Republic might need—a very respectable order to be given in one day. The Oroya Railway was to be 145 miles in length, and to cost 27,600,000 dols. To Puno the length was to be 232 miles from Arequipa, and the cost 35,000,000 dols. From Mollendo to Arequipa, 12,000,000

' Mr. Meiggs—"Whatever he obtained in Peru he has fully earned, and whatever he owed there or elsewhere he has paid. He has not been a seeker of contracts. On the contrary, he has rejected contracts that the Government wished him to take."'

dols., the length being 107 miles[1]. Ilo to Moquiqua, 63 miles, 6,700,000 dols. Pacasmayo to Caxamarca, or Guadalupe, or Magdalena, 83 miles, 7,700,000 dols. Payto to Piura, 63 miles. Chimbote to Huaraz, 172 miles, 40,000,000 dols.

Immediately after this small order was given, and Meiggs began to fill the world with the sound of his name, the Lima editors commenced their fulsome and disgusting eloquence, which day by day held all people in suspense. 'As puissant as colossal are the labours of the administration of Col. Don José Balta, who, without offence be it said, has a monomania for the construction of railways and public works—the infirmity of a divine inspiration in a head of the State.'

What the infirmity of a divine inspiration may be we will not stay to enquire. Goldsmith was called an inspired idiot: and perhaps this was what the learned editor meant to say of Col. Balta.

He goes on: 'The administration of Balta has converted the nation into a workshop. We say it in his honour that he has constructed rather than governed; but he has constructed well

[1] To which may be added $2,000,000 more for the conveyance of water along the line nearly from Arequipa to Mollendo.

and firmly. He has done more than this, he has created and conserved the habit of work in all the nation, demonstrating by the argument of deeds that revolutions spring principally from idleness.' 'Balta has cast a net of railways over the country which has taken anarchy captive. Without any difficulty might it be argued that the time of Balta will be the Octavian Era of Peru[1].'

Enough of this. Suffice it to say that among all these oratorical colonels, generals, lawyers, ministers of state, and accomplished editors, there was not one who had the honesty or the pluck to stand up and declare that it was all false which had so eloquently been said of the Oroya and the Arequipa Railways. They are neither the railways of the age nor of the day. There is one short railway in South America, the construction of which called forth more skill, pluck, and endurance than all the Meiggs railways put together, and this one railway has already earned in the first quarter of the century of its existence more money than all the government railways will ever earn during the next age. Hundreds of these inflated colonels and generals, judges, ministers of state, and accom-

[1] Ferrocarril de Arequipa, pp. lxxxi-ii.

plished editors, must have passed over the railway, which, running through a tropical forest, connects the Pacific with the Atlantic Ocean. Meiggs himself must have known it well; but neither he nor any of the inspired idiots who drowned him in butter had the valour to make mention of it by one poor word. The bridge over the Chagres river is of more utility, as it will win more enduring fame, than all the bridges on the Oroya, including those which 'are sixteen thousand feet above the level of the sea.' The Oroya bridges bear the same relation to those on the Panama Railway as the feat of the man who walked across the Falls of Niagara bears to the economy of walking. As Blondin was the only man who made any profit out of that performance, so Meiggs, the Messiah of railways, will be the only person who will for some time to come profit by the building of the Oroya and Lima line of railway. It is surely impossible that all the reports one has been compelled to give ear to of great silver mines and mines of copper existing on this line can be false. Yet mining, especially in Peru, is not free from danger; it is also not a little mixed up with lying and cheating, and it has a historical reputation for exaggeration. The copper mines on the Chimbote line, however, are quite another matter. If those on the Oroya can be demonstrated to be equally good, and the silver mines only half as good and as great, Peru may yet lift up her head. But he will be a bold man that shall apply to English capitalists for the first loan to Peruvian miners or to be invested in Peruvian mines, and the days of faith and trust will not have passed away when the money shall have been subscribed.

Although it was a poet who said that

'Borrowing dulls the edge of husbandry,'

yet it is as true as if it had emanated from the Stock Exchange, the *Times* monetary article, or any other recognised fountain of practical knowledge; and as for the native edge of Peruvian industry, it is about as dull as that of a razor not made to shave but to sell—as dull, in fact, as the edge of a hatchet made of lead.

## CHAPTER VI.

GUANO, Nitrate, and Railways being recognised as the prime sources of Peruvian greatness, and these having been noticed with no scant justice, another matter remains for examination, which may be said to surpass all the others in importance, albeit it is not so easy to estimate or understand.

Granted that Peru has all the physical elements of a great nation,—such as gold and silver, copper and iron, and coal, oil and wine, a vast line of sea-coast with numerous safe bays and ports, rivers for internal navigation, as well as railroads,—has she the moral qualities to develop these riches and make the best use of them? In plain words, has Peru ceased to be a hotbed of revolution? is there any hope that the ruling classes of the Peruvian people will become sober, industrious, thrifty, honest, just and right in all their dealings, and cease to be a source of anxiety and disgust to their present and future creditors?

These may be said to be momentous questions, and not to be lightly answered. Any answer not founded on well-ascertained facts and indisputable knowledge should be set aside as vexatious and frivolous. A hasty answer, or one founded on aught else, could only be conceived in malice or prompted by motives of self-interest. It has, for example, during the past few months been comparatively easy to a portion of the London press to defame the character of Peru; to find reasons why its bonds should be held only as waste paper, and even to prove to the satisfaction of its fond and eager readers that she is in an utterly bankrupt state. The same accomplished writers, if it suited their purpose, could as easily prove, with their eloquent persuasiveness, that Peru after all is, in commercial phraseology, sound; she had never yet failed in keeping faith with her English friends, and is too enlightened to think of doing so now. True, she is in debt; but she can pay handsomely, and, in the powerful rhetoric of Bassanio, would encourage money-lenders and her private friends thus:—

> 'In my school days, when I had lost one shaft,
> I shot his fellow of the self-same flight
> The self-same way with more advised watch,
> To find the other forth, and by adventuring both
> I oft found both. I urge this childhood proof,
> Because what follows is pure innocence.
> I owe you much, and, like a wilful youth,
> That which I owe is lost; but if you please
> To shoot another arrow that self way
> Which you did shoot the first, I do not doubt
> As I will watch the aim, or to find both
> Or bring your latter hazard back again
> And thankfully rest debtor for the first.'

But not thus will our serious questions meet with satisfactory answers.

The first thing to be noted in the enquiry, perhaps, is that it is altogether a misnomer to call Peru a Republic. Whatever else it be, a Republic it certainly is not, and never has been a Republic. Its political constitution and its laws have nothing whatever to do with the people, nor have the people aught to do with them; and they care for them as they care for the theory of gravitation, or any other portion of demonstrable knowledge, from which they may indeed derive some animal comfort in its application, but the application of which will probably never enlighten their souls. The people of Peru know as much of liberty as they know of the Virgin Mary. The priests once or twice a year dress the image of the Jewish maiden in tawdry attire, put a tinsel crown on her head, and call her the Mother of God and the Queen of Heaven, and the people fall down and worship; which they are perfectly at liberty to do, as the impostors who lead them to do so may get their living in that way, as all other impostors obtain theirs who possess the people's grace. In like fashion, all that the people know of liberty they know thus. They know as much of it as an aristocrat cares to teach them—as a quack can tell his patient of medicine, or the showy proprietress of a showy school can teach an intelligent girl the use of the globes. All native-born Peruvians of full age have votes, at least all such as can read and write, or possess a certain amount of real property. But reading and writing are not by any means universal accomplishments in the Peruvian Republic, and there are fewer holders of real estate among the working classes than maybe found in Barbados among the coloured labourers of that beautiful but misgoverned island.

Don Juan Espinosa, an old Peruvian soldier, and one of the few South American writers whose literary works have been translated into French, if not also into English, wrote some twenty years ago a republican, democratic, moral, political, and philosophical dictionary for the people. Strange to say, he has given us no definition of a Republic in his highly-entertaining and instructive book. Two of his longest articles, however, are devoted, the first to the subject of 'Independence,' and the second to 'Revolution.' The manner in which the author concludes the first is suggestive : 'On one day,' he says, 'we were all brothers and countrymen; brothers by blood, and countrymen of a land which we had just irrigated with our blood. O day immortal for humanity! On this day the Saviour of the world beheld the consummation of his work; he saw the spectacle which years before had led the way for 1824. He without doubt designed the camp of AYACUCHO as the first embrace of all the races, and the signal also for the suppression of all human rivalries. Afterwards'

———————————————————

A long, broad black line stretches across the page as if to put it in mourning.

'A revolution in substance,' he says, 'is nothing more than the organisation of a people's discontent.'

If that be so, there has never been a revolution in Peru; a statement which will be doubted by nearly all who hear it for the first time. We may perhaps make an exception in the revolution which made Col. Prado dictator of Peru in November, 1865. No doubt the enthusiasm of the Peruvian people for going to war with Spain was genuine, and Prado, not at all a man of revolutionary tastes, easily overthrew Canseco, because of his Spanish tendencies. Prado was subsequently elected President in 1867, but was overthrown by Balta and Canseco the year following, and Colonel (now General) Prado fled to Chile for his life. Still, let us be thankful that we can find one authentic instance of Peruvian patriotism in the course of fifty years, and that out of the hundreds of revolutions which have occurred, one was for the good of the country—and most certainly to its honour.

The anniversary of the 2nd of May, 1866, is kept with pride by every loyal Peruvian in all parts of the world, wherever one may find himself. Had there been among the Peruvian soldiers on that day as much knowledge of gunnery as there was of personal valour, not more than one or two ships of the Spanish fleet which bombarded Callao had escaped destruction.

It has been contended by a few anxious Peruvians that the revolution made by General Castilla, in 1854, against General Echenique was also a popular revolution. Perhaps it was. Echenique was notoriously very fond of money, and it is said that so freely did he help himself to the proceeds of the public guano that the people rose against him, flocked to the standard of Castilla, whom they kept in power for twelve years, and sent Echenique into ignoble exile. If that could be proved in favour of the Peruvian people, it should be done at once. But no one from sheer laughter can discuss the question. Castilla was as fond of money as Echenique; Castilla, however, did one or two liberal things; he liberated the slaves, and abolished the poll-tax, and in that sense the revolution of 1854 may be said to have been a popular one.

No Peruvian who supported those two famous acts of General Castilla's Government looks back upon them with anything but bitter regret. The negro slaves were well off—they were, moreover, a people with much affection for their masters, and slavery existed only in name. When the blacks, however, were 'liberated,' they became like a mob of mules without, burdens, without guide or master, and they wandered about the earth and died miserably. Those who survived were certainly very little credit to their friends, for many of them became the terror of the highways which converge on the capital of the Republic.

The Indians who paid the poll-tax did then do some work, and they were made to feel some of the responsibilities of being republicans—they were kept under rule—they could be induced to labour in 'some of the richest silver mines in the world.' Now they will do nothing of the kind, and the Government has not only lost an income of 2,000,000 dols. a year, they have lost the services of the entire indigenous population, which may be called, in classical language, a pretty kettle of fish, especially for a country whose riches depend upon the industry of a free and happy people.

One immediate consequence of Castilla's emancipation policy was that it speedily became a profitable business for a few adventurous persons in Lima to proceed to China, where they kidnapped some of the superfluous Chinese population. This traffic prospered for a while, but as it is the property of murder to make itself known—somehow or anyhow—the profits fell off, owing to the interference of one or two civilised Governments. When the Celestial Empire no longer offered a safe field for the Peruvian men-snatchers, attempts were made on the inoffensive people of the diocese of modern evangelisation, and in the course of time the rich people of Lima had the opportunity of buying a few men, women, and girls, who had been stolen from some of the islands of the Pacific. But these for some mysterious reasons died off, after having cost the Peruvian Government a serious sum of money, and some people their reputation. It was, however, imperatively necessary, owing to the demands of the British farmer for guano, and the exigences of the Government of Peru to obtain men from China somehow for the important work of shovelling Peruvian dung into European ships; and there may be reckoned to-day among the motley population of the Republic not less than 60,000 men who cultivate sugar and pig-tails, and indulge in opium. This, therefore, might be called a popular revolution, and the friends of General Castilla can claim for him the honour and glory of having brought it about.

General Castilla deserves to be better known; but this is not the place to speak of him at any length. He introduced a new era into Peruvian politics—he was the first native Peruvian with no Spanish blood in his veins who assumed supreme power. If there had been no guano to demoralise everybody, himself included, Castilla might have become a great man, and the Peruvian people been lifted up by him in the scale of humanity. As it is, Castilla and everybody else fulfilled the prediction of the Hebrew prophet in a manner that might be stated in Spanish, but which no gentleman can write in English. It should be stated that although Castilla had nothing of Spanish blood in his veins, yet his father was an Italian, and his mother one of the pure Indian women of Moquegua.

All this, however, does not help us to answer the momentous questions with which this chapter opens.—If Peru is not a Republic, and there have not been more than two revolutions in the whole of its wild and chequered history, what is it?

Peru is a Republic in name, 'governed' or rather farmed by groups or families of despots, who frequently quarrel among themselves, cut each other's throats, and alternately embrace and kiss each other, in a manner that is sickening to any one who is not a moral eunuch[1]. Only those who are rich enough to escape to Chile are saved from the above gentle process. General Prado is one of these favoured Peruvians. Had not Don Manuel Pardo, the late President, fled from Lima during the revolting days of the Gutierrz terror, he too would have gone the way of all flesh and Peruvian political farmers.

The people of Peru, those who are to be distinguished from the families who farm them, are hard-working, industrious, sober, ignorant, excitable and superstitious. They are fond of serving their masters, they like to be called 'children' by the great Colonels, the great sugar-boilers, and all who ride on horses and live, even though it be at other people's expense, in great houses.

The Peruvian dictionary already quoted from, though it does not contain the word Republic, does contain the history of Peru. Let us turn to the article 'Liberty.'

'LA LIBERTAD,' says our brave soldier author,

[1] *Estratocracia* I find is the technical term by which Espinosa would designate the Government of Peru or a government by the military. This would seem to be true, seeing that since Peru became a Republic all its Presidents with only one exception have been Colonels, Generals, and Field Marshals.

'does not consist, civilly or socially speaking, in each one doing what he likes. By thus understanding liberty some governments have fallen, and some people have lost what they had gained.

'Liberty consists in each one having the power to do, at all events, that which the law has not forbidden, in not damaging another in his rights, or property, or in his moral and material well-being.

'That society is not free while any of its members are unable to express their thoughts without hinderance.

'That society is not free when one or more of its industries are prohibited under the pretext of monopoly or privilege.

'It is not free when it cares not, or is unable to arraign a lying magistrate.

'That society is not free which does not possess political morality. This consists in—

'I. Keeping the treaties and covenants made with other nations.

'II. In submitting to the law without its ever supposing itself entitled to falsify it by cunning arts, or paltry subterfuge.

'III. In holding up to scorn whatever crime affects the national honour.

'IV. In not corrupting its institutions for personal considerations. A people will find it very difficult to maintain its freedom, which is without sufficient spirit to provide itself with good institutions, and afterwards ready to put so much faith in them, that it will become a religious duty rigorously to support them.

'By what right does Spanish-America call itself republican, if it has not renounced the custom of a despotic monarchical absolutism?

'These unhappy people have given themselves very liberal laws, and have afterwards abandoned them at the caprice of men without having the least faith in their own institutions.

'How can they thus hope to be free?

'It costs nothing, nor is it of any value to shout LIBERTY, LIBERTY. But that which is of great price, and can never be too costly, is to acquire liberty by means of good manners, by the custom of respecting the law and making it respected, by respecting the rights of others, and making them respected by all; to be just with all the world, and ashamed of every evil act. Behold, how liberty is to be acquired. In fine, liberty is the health of the soul, and he cannot be free who has not a healthy conscience.'

'The greater number of our liberals,' he adds in another place, with one of his happiest flashes of poetic truth, of which the book is full, 'the greater number of our liberals are like musical instruments which do not retain the sound they give when played upon,' i. e. they are cracked.

Let it be added, that this soldier of the sword and of the pen who fought and bled on the field of battle for Peruvian civil liberty, and sighed, and cried in peaceful days for a freedom still greater and better, died poor and neglected. The present Peruvian Government sought all over Lima for complete copies of his works to send to Philadelphia, but it allows those whom he has left behind him, and who bear his name, to languish in obscurity and in want; and Don Manuel Pardo and his ministers, good in many things though they may be, are in others nothing better than cracked musical instruments. Peru is only a Republic in name, liberty does not exist, its people are not free, and the country remains at the mercy of men who at any moment, and in the most unexpected manner, can turn it into a hotbed of what is called revolution.

A revolution is expected now. The man whose administration designed and carried through one of the 'railways of the age,' the personal friend of Meiggs, who had taken anarchy captive in an iron net, was shortly afterwards in the most cowardly, brutal, and unexpected way first made prisoner, while he was yet President, and then murdered in his jail.

Great as is the love of the common people for their superiors, they are not to be relied upon in days of great excitement, and when there is abundance of loose change flying about. How could it be otherwise?

How often do ministers and public men meet the people in common? Never, except in a religious procession carrying an enormous wax candle a yard long, and as thick as a rolling-pin, or at the Theatre on el dos de Mayo, and not then unless there has been some pleasant news announced the day before.

How often are the people enlightened by a clear and straightforward statement of the public accounts? Never. Does not the free press of Lima support the Government, or now and then criticise its acts in the interest of the people? The answer is that there is no free press in Lima.

No plan of the Government is ever made known until it has been accomplished. Everything is done in secret and underground.

Rumour is the great agent of the Government and mystery its chief force. So mysterious are the ways of the Executive that itself is not unfrequently a mystery to itself. No Peruvian Government has ever had the courage to take the people into its confidence, and the people are too busy with their own personal affairs to think of, much less to resent, the slight.

In other matters the press is busy enough. Some of the most biting criticisms on priests, on auricular confession, on the infallibility of the Pope and the Immaculate Conception have appeared in the Lima press. Their teachers, in brief, have ridiculed the gods of the people and given them none to adore. No intellectual society in Lima associate with priests. No priest is ever seen in the houses of the rich, or the respectable poor.

Freemasonry is the fashionable religion of men, and men who never go to mass will frequent a lodge twice a week. Only the other day one of these lodges published an advertisement in the leading journal to the effect that a gold medal would be conferred on any brother mason who would adopt the orphan child of any who had died fighting against any form of tyranny, and the medal is to be worn as a badge of honour on the person of the owner. Freemasonry in Peru is an open menace of the Church, which with all deference to the craft, may be called a gross mistake. But Peruvian Freemasonry is like Peruvian Republicanism, chiefly a thing of show, and something to talk about by men who can talk of nothing else.

After all this it should not be difficult to answer the questions with which this chapter opens.

But lest it should be thought that the greater part of these statements is pure rhetoric, or mere private opinion, and not stubborn facts, let us now ask two questions more.

What use has Peru made of the great income it has derived during the past generation, from the national guano? What is there to show for the many million pounds sterling it has derived from this source, and from money lent by English bondholders?

Let us hasten at once to acknowledge that it has spent 150,000,000 dols. in railways. But let us also add that the greatest authority in Peru has stigmatised these railways as *locuras*, or follies. This is not an encouraging beginning. But alas it is not only the beginning, it is also the end of the account.

There is nothing else to be seen. There is not a single lighthouse or light on any dangerous rock, or at any port difficult to make along the whole of its coast. All the fructifying rivers of the hills still steal into the sea. Had half the money which has been spent on the Oroya railway been expended on works of irrigation, the Government of Peru would now be in the possession of a respectable revenue.

A morning visit to the market-place in Lima on any day of the week, is enough to convince even a Peruvian President who knows something else besides how to play rocambor, of the truth of this statement.

Internal roads, excepting these 'railways of the age,' there are none; but there are several ironclads and men-of-war in the Bay of Callao, for what use or of what service the First Lord of the Admiralty himself could not tell explicitly.

It might be thought by some ordinary people, of business habits and a little reflection, that a country like Peru, which can boast of as many seaports as it can of first-class towns and cities, would provide those ports with convenient landing-places, moles, or piers.

There is one good pier on the whole coast,

which in its useless grandeur stretches out nearly a mile into the sea; as the Oroya railway, like a mighty python, creeps up the precipitous slopes of the Andes 'sixteen thousand feet above the level of the sea.'

As every one knows, the Pacific is a peaceful sea, as quiet as a saucer of milk. But like almost all the things that every one knows, this piece of knowledge will hardly bear the test of experience. Twenty miles or less from its shore, the Pacific on the Peruvian coast, may be said to be as calm and placid as a man's unresisted vices. Put a restraint upon, or raise a barrier against the most modest of the man's wishes, and these suddenly show their strength, even the strength, as some have found to their cost, of resistless passion. It is thus with this Pacific sea. When it comes against a rocky shore, or the miserable wooden barriers which the Peruvian Government have put up for the convenience and comfort of passengers, and the despatch of business, it becomes more like a wild beast, or a watery volcano, or any other fierce and angry force which cannot by ordinary means be restrained. It is not unlikely that a Government fond of providing cheap distraction for the people has purposely neglected this useful work of building piers, with the benevolent design of providing a cheap amusement to those inhabitants of the ports who do not travel by sea.

It is such fun to see a lady dressed in pink satin and blue silk boots get a sudden ducking in salt water, or to watch in safety from the shore a boat full of anxious and highly dressed colonels and sugar-boilers, editors and lawyers, get drenched to the skin, and almost robbed of their breath, in trying to effect a landing at Islay, or Mollendo, Iquique, or Chala, or even Callao.

If any of the readers of this brief but eventful history would desire to see the Peruvian Republic as in a microcosm, let them arrive at the latter chief port of the nation in a steamer, or a cattle ship, as a passenger steamer may now be called. They will see an exhibition of confusion, extortion, bullying, insolence, cruelty, and official imbecility, which cannot be equalled in any other part of the civilised or uncivilised world, including New Guinea or Eragomanga. And as it is now, so it was twenty years ago. A steamer, the European mail for example, drops its anchor about two miles from the shore. It is then surrounded by a hundred small boats, each containing two, sometimes more, coloured men. The screaming, gesticulating, and brutal language of these creatures defy description. The authorities have no control over them, the captain of the steamer is powerless against the invasion of his ship, and all passengers who have no friends, who know nothing of the country and cannot speak Spanish, are placed at the mercy of this swarm of harpies.

Here you have an epitome of Peru. Gentlemen and rogues jostling one another in painful contiguity. Gentlewomen and their opposite, men who work and scoundrels who prey upon other people's labour, priests and colonels, knowledge and ignorance, in some form or other brought in violent collision: the utmost freedom of opinion and nobody to keep the peace!

www.ingramcontent.com/pod-product-compliance
Lightning Source LLC
Chambersburg PA
CBHW030310170426
43202CB00009B/947